海之龙：利物浦和她的中国海员

SEA DRAGONS: LIVERPOOL AND ITS CHINESE SEAMEN

[英] 查尔斯·弗雷德里克·威廉·弗利（Charles Frederick William Foley）
[英] 伊婉·玛格丽特·弗利（Yvonne Margaret Foley） 著
韩 庆 刘迎春 赵志垒 译

中国民主法制出版社

图书在版编目（CIP）数据

海之龙：利物浦和她的中国海员：汉英对照／（英）查尔斯·弗雷德里克·威廉·弗利，（英）伊婉·玛格丽特·弗利著；韩庆，刘迎春，赵志垒译．—北京：中国民主法制出版社，2019. 1

ISBN 978-7-5162-1973-7

Ⅰ．①海… Ⅱ．①查… ②伊… ③韩… ④刘… ⑤赵… Ⅲ．①华人－社区－历史－研究－利物浦－汉、英 Ⅳ．①D756. 183

中国版本图书馆 CIP 数据核字（2019）第 022575 号

图书出品人：刘海涛
全 案 统 筹：乔先彪
责 任 编 辑：陈 曦 姜园园

书 名／SEA DRAGONS：LIVERPOOL AND ITS CHINESE SEAMEN
海之龙：利物浦和她的中国海员
作 者／［英］查尔斯·弗雷德里克·威廉·弗利（Charles Frederick William Foley）
［英］伊婉·玛格丽特·弗利（Yvonne Margaret Foley） 著
韩 庆 刘迎春 赵志垒 译

出 版·发 行／中国民主法制出版社
地 址／北京市丰台区玉林里 7 号（100069）
电 话／（010）63055259（总编室） 63057714（发行部）
传 真／（010）63056975 63056983
http：//www. npcpub. com
E-mail：mzfz@ npcpub. com
经 销／新华书店
开 本／32 开 880 毫米×1230 毫米
印 张／8. 625 **字数**／182 千字
版 本／2019 年 3 月第 1 版 2019 年 3 月第 1 次印刷
印 刷／北京中兴印刷有限公司

书 号／ISBN 978-7-5162-1973-7
定 价／35. 00 元

本书由：

中央高校基本科研业务费项目“海洋历史文化与战略研究”

与教育部哲学社会科学研究重大课题攻关项目“中外海洋文化交流历史文献的整理与传播研究”

资助出版。

CONTENTS

目　录

01

Chapter 1. In the beginning

第一章　写在前面

Liverpool's Anglo-Chinese community owed its existence to three things that were happening at around the same time. One was the long, slow and painful death of the Chinese Empire. Then the later warlordism made the life of people more and more difficult. some of them selected to work on foreign ships. The second was the invention by Alfred Holt, a Liverpool ship owner, of a marine steam engine far more efficient than anything else available up to that time. Many Holt`s ships appeared on the far east line and monopolized it. The third was the abolition in 1849 of the British Navigation Acts. The Navigation Acts which required that 75 percent of the crew of a British merchant vessel be British sailors. So Chinese would have more opportunity to work on British Ships.

The way was now open for increasing trade with China. What is more, it could now be carried out in efficient steam powered ships and those ships could be manned by cheap and efficient Chinese crews.

The background

Qianlong, the last great Chinese Emperor had been dead (died) for over 40 years when, in 1840, the British broke down the doors of the Middle Kingdom and took the island of Hong Kong. By then it had been half a century since the trade mission to China led by the Earl of McCartney had been told by Qianlong 'We possess all things...and have no need of your country's

利物浦华人社区的形成大致归因于在同一时期发生的三件事情。一是中华帝国在漫长的苦苦挣扎中走向覆灭，之后的军阀混战使中国百姓的生活日益困苦，从而使一些人选择在外国商船上工作。二是利物浦的船东阿尔弗雷德·霍尔特发明了一种船用蒸汽机，比当时同类产品效率更高，于是越来越多的霍尔特公司的船舶出现在远东航线，并且进一步垄断了这条航线。三是 1849 年英国废除了《航海法案》。该法案此前规定，一艘英国商船上 75% 的船员必须是英国籍海员，这样一来，中国人有更多的机会在英国商船上工作。

这样一来，中英贸易逐渐增加。重要的是，船舶广泛使用高效的蒸汽机，并且船东可以雇佣到廉价称职的中国船员。

背 景

1840 年，在中国最后一个伟大统治者乾隆驾崩 40 多年后，英国强行打开了中华帝国的门户，强占香港岛。半个世纪前，马戛尔尼伯爵率领的英国贸易代表团访问中国时，乾隆皇帝曾对他们说过："天朝物产丰盈，无所不有，原不藉（借）外夷货物以通有无。"事实上，中国不仅仅对英国关闭了贸易的大门，也将世界其他国家拒之门外。中国自给自足的自然经济对外国商品有很强的抵御力，早期中英贸易中，中国长期处于贸

manufactures.'[①] In effect, slamming the door in the face of not just the British but any other country that wished to trade with China. China's Self-sufficient natural economy has a strong resistance to foreign goods, in the early Sino-British trade, China was in long-term trade surplus position, so the British began to bring opium to China to offset the trade deficit. They had a ready supply of it from its Indian colony and began shipping it into China in ever-increasing quantities.

By the 1840s the rapid growth of the opium trade was inflicting significant damage on the Chinese Empire both economically and socially. Attempts by the Chinese Government to stifle the trade led to war with Britain. A war that the British won easily with their state of the art warships and military hardware.

The Chinese were humiliated and forced to sign the first of what, to this day, the Chinese Government call 'The Unequal Treaties'. Hong Kong was handed over to Britain and a series of other towns were opened to the victors as centres for trade. Among them Shanghai and Ningbo – places that, along with Hong Kong, would be of key importance for the formation of Liverpool's Anglo-Chinese community,[②] most of the Chinese building up the Anglo-Chinese community in the coming days would come from these ports.

---

① Singer, A. 'The Lion and the Dragon', Barrie and Jenkins, London 1992, Appendix A Edict from the Emperor Qianlong to King George III, pp.180 – 182.

② Spence, J.D. 'The Search for Modern China', W. W. Norton and Company, London 1999, pp.160 – 162.

易顺差地位，于是英国商人开始向中国输入鸦片以抵消贸易逆差，在印度殖民地种植了大量可以随时供应的现货，并且开始源源不断地运向中国。

到了19世纪40年代，鸦片贸易的急速增长给中华帝国的经济和社会造成了巨大的损失。清政府试图遏制鸦片贸易，却导致了中英鸦片战争。英国凭借着先进的战舰和军事装备，轻而易举地取得了战争的胜利。

清政府被迫签订了第一个不平等条约，香港被割让给英国，一系列城市被迫开放成为战胜国的贸易中心。其中上海、宁波、香港等口岸对于利物浦英华社区的形成起到了至关重要的作用，后来构建利物浦英华社区的中国人大多来自这些口岸。

By the 1860s the decay of the Chinese Empire had progressed to the point where it was being wracked by Taiping or Heavenly Peace Rebellion that was to cost tens of millions of lives. A civil war that was itself a by-product of the opening of China to the West. Christian missionaries now had access to China and its teeming population and soon began to make converts, particularly among the poor and the marginalised. The Hakka were just such a group. Originating in the north of China, these so-called 'guest people' had been living in the southern Province of Guangdong for centuries. The province of which Hong Kong had been a part before the British took the island.

One young Hakka man, Hong Xiuquan, had been exposed to the teachings of the missionaries now operating more or less freely in the Empire. After repeatedly failing in the examinations for the Imperial Civil Service he had what can only be described as a nervous breakdown. He became convinced that he was the Son of God, the brother of Christ.[①] Setting out to make converts amongst the oppressed Hakka, he was soon leading a rebellion against the Empire. This so-called Taiping or Heavenly Peace Rebellion would last for over a decade and devastate vast areas of Northern China. It would even lap at the very edges of what was by then the British run city of Shanghai. Not only did millions die in this conflict but millions more were left in what would be for us in the modern and affluent West a state of unimaginable poverty and desperation.

① Spence, J.D. 'God's Chinese Son: the Taiping Heavenly Kingdom of Hong Xiuquan', Harper Collins, London 1996 Foreword p. ix.

到了 19 世纪 60 年代，衰败的中华帝国在太平天国运动的打击下支离破碎，加速走向覆灭，数千万人死于战争。这场战争便是中国对西方国家开放门户所带来的副作用。基督教传教士可以到中国传教，随后大量中国人的信仰开始转变，尤其是在穷人和边缘化人群之中。客家族便是这样的一个群体，客家族来自中国北部，但此前这些所谓的“客家人”已在南方的广东省生活了几个世纪。香港岛在被割让给英国之前便是广东省的一部分。

当时基督教已经可以在中华帝国更加自由地传播，一名年轻的客家人洪秀全接触到了基督教的教义。在经历了几次科举考试落榜后，他的精神崩溃了，但他坚信自己是上帝之子、耶稣的兄弟，并开始游说深受压迫的客家人做他的门徒。因此他很快就领导了一场反抗清王朝的起义，也就是太平天国运动。太平天国运动持续了十余年之久，给中国北方[①]广袤的土地带来了巨大的摧残。战局甚至一度扩大到了英国商人云集的上海市边缘。不仅数以百万计的生命消逝于这场战争之中，更将数以百万计的百姓置于贫穷与绝望之中，这是现代且富裕的西方国家难以想象的。

① 相对于广东而言。——译者注

It was more or less at this point that Alfred Holt enters the story. His efficient new marine steam engine was a true technological breakthrough. Its invention meant that a vessel no longer had to carry so much coal that there was not enough space to load a profitable cargo. It meant that his ships could sail all the way around the world to China and do so at a price that undercut his rivals. This would help to make him a very rich man.①

But it was not just his new engine that gave Alfred Holt an advantage. The other key element in his simple but very effective formula for success was that he began to employ Chinese seamen. Cheaper by far than their British counterparts and far more reliable, they had been used by the British since at least the time of the Napoleonic Wars. Then they had been recruited to replace British seamen taken into the Royal Navy. And, as we shall see, that was to happen again in the twentieth century in both the First and Second World Wars.

For the British recruiting Chinese mariners made sense. They did not drink alcohol and become violent or utterly incapacitated as the British seamen did. Their diet made them immune from the scurvy that killed or debilitated most European crews on long voyages. The Chinese made good seamen and China had a long and proud maritime history. They had been travelling the world long before Europe was even aware that most of it existed.

In the fifteenth century the Chinese Emperor had sent out vast

① Craggs, S and Lynn, I Loh 'A History of Liverpool's Chinese Community', Merseyside Community Relations Council, Liverpool, 1985, pp.1 – 2.

大约在这一时期，阿尔弗雷德·霍尔特登上了历史舞台。他发明的新型高效船用蒸汽机是一项货真价实的技术突破。这项发明意味着船上不再需要装载过多的煤炭，可以腾出更多的空间装载盈利的货物。同时也意味着他的船舶可以经世界各地航行到中国，而且运费远远低于竞争对手，因此他发了大财。

阿尔弗雷德·霍尔特的成功并不仅仅是因为他发明了新型的蒸汽机，另一个让他成功的关键因素就是他开始雇佣中国海员。英国人自从拿破仑战争时期就开始雇佣中国海员，因为中国海员比英国海员更加廉价也更加可靠。于是中国海员便替代了英国皇家海军征召的那些英国海员。并且正如我们看到的那样，这种情况在20世纪的第一次世界大战、第二次世界大战中也普遍存在。

英国人雇佣中国海员是有道理的，因为中国海员不会像英国海员那样，因为酗酒而暴力相向，或者完全丧失适任能力。另外，中国船员的饮食使得他们对坏血病完全免疫，而在远航中，坏血病对于大多数欧洲海员来说却是严重的威胁，甚至是致命的。中国船员久负盛名，其航海历史悠久而令人自豪。在欧洲人意识到大部分世界存在之前，中国海员一直在环球航行。

15世纪时，中国皇帝派遣大量船队探索世界，并宣示强权与财力。在中国航海家郑和的带领下，中国舰队环游了世界

fleets to explore the world and demonstrate the power and wealth of China. Under the eunuch Admiral Zheng He the Chinese had, so some writers believe, discovered the Americas and Australia, sailed around the world and drawn the maps that Europeans were to use in the centuries ahead in their own 'discoveries'.[①] The Chinese seamen that Alfred Holt was to recruit were the heirs to a great tradition.

But in the poor and chaotic China of the mid-nineteenth century the power and might of centuries past was a long distant memory. The China that faced Alfred Holt was one that provided him with an almost unlimited supply of willing and desperate labour. From Hong Kong and surrounding Guangdong Province tough and strong young peasants had already been flooding out to the gold fields of California and Australia over the previous decade. They were working to build the American railroads and would be shipped out as virtual slave labour to South America and anywhere else that would take them. For almost the next 100 years they would provide Holt's Blue Funnel Line with its deckhands. The men who would work on deck in all weathers. The men that young Fred Bishop[②] would remember so well for their courage in the storm that so damaged his ship.

But Alfred Holt also had available to him skilled and experienced seamen. Recruiting in Shanghai he had access to

① Menzies, G. '1421: the Year China Discovered the World', Transworld Publishers, London, 2002, pp. 3 – 12.

② Fred Bishop was an old seaman who got in touch with Yvonne to tell her about this story.

并且画出了世界地图。[1]几个世纪以后，欧洲人才通过“地理大发现”绘制出了类似的地图，因此有些作家相信郑和才是发现美洲大陆和澳洲大陆的第一人。阿尔弗雷德·霍尔特雇佣的中国海员继承了这样的优良传统。

19世纪中期的中国，处在一个既贫穷又混乱的时期，过去几个世纪以来强大威严的帝国已经是一段遥远的回忆了。阿尔弗雷德·霍尔特面对的便是这样的中国，其为他提供了源源不断的劳工，这些劳工饱受绝望的折磨，从而心甘情愿地为他工作。在过去的10年里，来自香港和广东一带年轻力壮的农民不断涌向美国加利福尼亚州和澳大利亚的金矿。实际上，等待他们的是到美国去修建铁路或者被运到南美或是其他任何愿意接收他们的地方当苦力。在接下来的近100年时间里，他们又在霍尔特的蓝烟囱轮船公司担任普通水手，就是无论什么天气都要在甲板上工作的水手。虽然猛烈的暴风雨摧毁了船只，但中国水手们面对风暴的勇气令年轻的弗雷德·毕晓普[2]铭记于心，印象深刻。

阿尔弗雷德·霍尔特还在中国找到了技术娴熟并且经验丰富的海员。在上海雇佣船员的时候，他接触到了生活在海岛岸边的渔民和他们的后代。这些渔民熟知海性和航路，他们在小

① 这种说法并不准确。中外部分学者认为郑和做过环球航行，但并无充分证据。

② 弗雷德·毕晓普是一名英国海员，曾和中国海员一起工作过，也是作者的朋友。——译者注

the fishermen and the sons of fishermen who lived on the islands off the coast. Men familiar with the sea and its ways. Men who had learned their craft in small boats and for whom Alfred Holt's vessels would seem like floating palaces. Over time, as Shanghai became China's industrial centre, it would be the skilled tradesmen and engineers from the city and from Ningbo that would keep the Blue Funnel vessels sailing from the UK to Australia and the Far East.

渔船上练就了一身技巧，因此阿尔弗雷德·霍尔特的船舶对他们来说就像是海上宫殿一般。随着时间的推移，上海成为了中国的工业中心，也正是得益于这些来自上海和宁波的有经验的商人和海员，"蓝烟囱"的船舶得以一路从英国驶向澳洲和远东。

02

Chapter 2. The Chinatown that never was

第二章　从未存在的唐人街

In the early twentieth century，mention the word 'Chinatown' to most people and the pictures that will appear in their minds will owe a lot to the American movies. Narrow alleys. Dark narrow alleys. For some reason, it is always night. People in strange costumes appear briefly from one of these alleys before slinking (they always slink) into another alley. There are glimpses, only glimpses, of exotic females in dresses slit up the sides who glance over the tops of their fans at us. And inscrutable men with pigtails. Chinese men are always inscrutable in this make-believe world. Of course, everyone wears either a broad brimmed straw hat or a silk skullcap, and they smoke opium.

In these cinematic versions of Chinatown there are seldom any white men. Except for a few hopeless cases addicted to the evil – opium. The only white women are those who have been sold into 'white slavery'. Poor creatures doomed to be the playthings of the evil yellow men. They too may be addicted to the dreaded opium.

Unfortunately for the myth, America's San Francisco Chinatown, on which the movies built this picture of a Chinese community, was almost unique. It owed its existence in the form on which the legends are based largely due to the coincidence of three main factors. Firstly, the employment of so many Chinese as labourers in the building of the American railroads. Second, it was possible to bring in Chinese women into the USA. Men who were merchants, or could convince the authorities that they were merchants, could

在20世纪初期，提到“唐人街”这个字眼，大多数人脑海中涌现出这样的画面：街道狭窄而且阴暗。这主要归因于美国电影，不知为什么，美国电影中唐人街的背景总是在晚上，身着奇装异服的人从一条巷子里鬼鬼祟祟地溜进另一条巷子里，而且他们总是鬼鬼祟祟的。而中国女人的身影总是一闪而过，她们身穿开衩到大腿的旗袍，手执着扇子半遮面颊，只露出眼睛扫视着行人。还有神秘莫测的男人梳着猪尾辫。在这个假想的世界里，中国男人总是神秘莫测，每个人都戴着一顶帽子，不是宽边的草帽，就是丝质的无檐帽，而且他们还抽鸦片。

在这些电影版的唐人街中很少会出现白人男性的身影，即使有，也是为数不多的几个染上了毒品鸦片的绝望的人。出现在唐人街的白人女性大多都是被卖作“白人奴隶”的可怜人，注定要沦为这些中国男人的玩物，而且她们也可能染上了致命的鸦片。

不过，这些传闻大多是假想，在美国旧金山唐人街的基础上，美国电影构建了一幅独一无二的华人社区画面。这类华人社区画面的形成可以大致归因于三个很巧合的因素：一是大量中国劳工被雇佣到美国修建铁路；二是他们可以将中国女人带到美国，那些商人或者能使美国政府相信自己是商人的男人，有能力也有财力把自己的妻子带到美国；三是旧金山华人社区的人大多都来自中国同一地区而且几乎讲同一种语言——广东话或者广东的某种方言。这些因素也为旧金山华人维系自己的文化和语言提供了基本条件。

bring their wives and had the money to do so.[①] The third factor was that the vast majority of the San Francisco community came from the same area of China and most spoke the same language – Cantonese or some dialect of Cantonese. This helped create the critical mass that enabled the Chinese in San Francisco to maintain their culture and language.

Well, Liverpool's Chinatown was never like that and few Chinatowns throughout the world were. Liverpool's Anglo-Chinese community was, in its way, typical of all Chinatown's outside of the USA. It consisted of a relatively small number of Chinese men, most of whom came to Liverpool as seamen on Holt ships. There were very few Chinese women and poorly paid merchant seamen did not have the finance to bring women out of China. Even if a Chinese mariner had the money, he would have faced the opposition of the Chinese authorities who for many years took precautions to stop women leaving China.[②]And after 1914 he would have found that he could only bring out a wife if she was over forty years of age.[③]The Aliens Restriction Act, deliberately or not, thus ensured that only women who would be unlikely to bear children could enter the country. So, if a young Chinese man in Liverpool wanted a family life, he had no choice but to marry a local girl.

---

① See, L. 'On Gold Mountain', Arrow, London, 1999, pp. 81 – 82.

② Blue, A.D. 'Chinese Emigration and the Deck Passenger Trade' in 'The Journal of the Hong Kong Branch of the Royal Asiatic Society', Vol.10, 1970, pp. 86 – 87.

③ Craggs, S and Lynn, I Loh 'A History of Liverpool's Chinese Community', Merseyside Community Relations Council, Liverpool, 1985, p.4.

然而，利物浦的唐人街却并非如此，世界上几乎没有几个唐人街是美国这样的。利物浦华人社区，在某些方面来说，是除了美国以外世界其他华人社区的典型代表。它由少数中国男人组成，这些人大多是霍尔特船上的船员。中国女人数量并不多，商船船员因为工资微薄，没有经济能力把自己的女人带出中国。即使一个中国船员有钱，他也会面临中国政府的反对，早在多年以前中国政府便采取措施禁止女人离开中国。1914年后，随着英国《外国人限制法案》的实施，中国船员只能将年过40岁的妻子带到英国。无论是否有意，该法案保证了只有无法继续生育的女人才能来到英国。因此，在利物浦如果一个年轻的中国男人想要结婚生子，除了与当地的女孩结婚外别无选择。

As to the men, they were always too few to attain the critical mass that San Francisco achieved. In 1906 the 'Liverpool Courier' newspaper mentions '…only 100 to 200…' Chinese in Liverpool.① And this was to be true for many years to come. From its earliest days up to its last flowering in World War Two there were seldom more than a few hundred. Only during the two World Wars, as we shall see, were there any significant numbers of Chinese men in the city. Even then they were split into different language groups. The deckhands spoke Cantonese but the engine room crew spoke Shanghai dialect. Two mutually incomprehensible languages that were and are as different as Italian and German.

In the second half of the 19th century, Liverpool's Chinatown was the usual mix that you get when young men are far from home, are not going back home and want to settle down. The same as Hong Kong and Shanghai, where it was young British men who were far from home, they settled down with local Chinese girls. We find that the British policemen in Hong Kong and Shanghai, the tradesmen working in the shipyards and the seamen who found local employment took Chinese partners.② Unlike the rich merchants living there who could bring wives out from the UK; these men did not have the finance to do so – just like the Chinese seamen in Liverpool.

① 'Liverpool's Chinatown: The Alleged Overcrowding – Statement by the Medical Officer' in 'The Liverpool Courier', Friday, December 7th, 1906, Liverpool Central Library, Liverpool, UK.

② Letherbridge, H.J. 'Conditions of the European Working Class in Nineteenth Century Hong Kong' in 'The Journal of the Hong Kong Branch of the Royal Asiatic Society' Vol.15, 1975, pp. 88 – 112.

利物浦不像旧金山，并没有足够多的华人。在1906年的《利物浦信使报》中提到，利物浦“只有100到200个”华人，并且这一情况在接下来的许多年里仍是如此。从最开始一直到第二次世界大战最后一次人口繁荣期时也不过几百人。正如我们所见，只有在两次世界大战期间利物浦的华人数量才有了明显的增加。但即使在那时，他们仍根据所使用的语言，分成不同的群体。甲板水手说广东话，轮机机工说上海方言。这两种发音不同的语言就如同意大利语和德语一样，相互难以理解。

从19世纪下半叶开始，利物浦的唐人街汇聚了背井离乡、不想回家和想要安定下来的年轻人。同样在香港和上海，远离家乡的英国年轻小伙会和当地的中国姑娘结婚定居。我们还会发现，在香港和上海的英国籍警察，以及在造船厂工作的英国籍商人，还有在本地找到工作的英国籍船员都会找个中国伴侣。这些人不同于生活在此的富有商人，可以把妻子从英国带出来，他们同在利物浦生活的华人海员一样，没有这样做的经济实力。

But who were the girls that they married or took as partners? Whether British or Chinese, these young women had much in common. A 'respectable' Chinese family would not want their daughter to marry a big nosed hairy barbarian.[①] The girls the young Brits married were those at the margins of Chinese society. The Hakka, the Tanka fisher women and the daughters of the poor.[②] None of these groups bound their daughters' feet. They could not afford crippled daughters and these girls made good and thrifty partners for their Western husbands.

In the same way, in Liverpool in the early twentieth century a girl marrying a non-white was likely to find herself rejected by her own family. So we find that the girls who did marry these foreigners were, like their Chinese counterparts, at the margins of society and with poor prospects. The young women were often Liverpool Irish.[③] Catholic by religion and at the bottom of the social scale. Unlikely to make a 'good' marriage in a city divided by religion and probably facing a life of filth, poverty and drunken violence when they did marry. Confronted with such a bleak future, the young Liverpool Irish girl was to see marriage to a Chinese man as something to be desired. Clean, a non-drinker, hard worker

---

① Coates, P.D. 'The Chinese Consuls: British Consular Officers 1843 – 1943' Oxford University Press, Hong Kong, 1988, p. 10.

② Letherbridge, H.J. 'Conditions of the European Working Class in Nineteenth Century Hong Kong' in 'The Journal of the Hong Kong Branch of the Royal Asiatic Society' Vol.15, 1975, p. 109.

③ Pan, L. 'Sons of the Yellow Emperor: the Story of the Overseas Chinese', Mandarin, London, 1991, pp. 156-157; Lee, G.B. 'Chinas Unlimited: Making Imaginaries of China and Chineseness', Routledge Curzon, London, 2003, p.92.

但他们迎娶的或选为终身伴侣的姑娘都是谁呢？诚然，一个体面的中国家庭是不会允许自己的女儿嫁给一个大鼻子、浑身长毛的“野蛮人”的。那些和年轻的英国小伙结婚的中国姑娘都来自中国社会的边缘群体：客家 (Hakka)、疍家 (Tanka) 的打渔女还有穷苦人家的女儿。这些群体里的人家都不会给女儿裹脚，因为他们抚养不起小脚女人。因此这些勤俭持家的姑娘就成了西方小伙的伴侣。

同样，在 20 世纪早期的利物浦，一个白人女性如果和其他肤色的人结婚通常都会遭到家人的反对。因此，我们不难发现那些与外国人结婚的英国姑娘同中国姑娘的情况一样，都是处于社会的边缘群体且前途堪忧。这些年轻的姑娘通常是爱尔兰裔利物浦人，信仰天主教而且处于社会阶级的最底层。由于宗教原因不太可能得到一份体面的婚姻，就算结婚了也很有可能过上肮脏、贫穷并且充斥着酗酒与家暴的生活。面对着这样暗淡的未来，这些年轻的爱尔兰裔利物浦姑娘将与中国男人结婚视为一件值得渴望的事情。中国男人爱干净、不喝酒、工作努力而且受文化影响是顾家的好男人。虽然他有可能是个赌徒，但是他仍然会照顾自己的孩子。

and culturally pre-disposed to be a good family man. He may well have been a gambler but he would take care of his children.[①]

2.1 Liverpool the melting pot

America always boasts that it is a melting pot of different ethnicities and cultures. To some extent this is true. Not quite as true as the Americans would have us believe with its racial tensions and self-imposed national and ethnic ghettoes. But Liverpool and Liverpudlians have always been like the city's favourite local dish, scouse, a mixture of what happens to be around. Predominantly English, Irish and Welsh but with a lot of added spice from Africa and Asia.[②]

The Liverpool accent owes much to the influx of desperate Irish who began coming during the Irish potato famine in the 1840s and who have kept coming ever since. Another nation of Celts have added their genes to the mix and their voices to the Liverpool Sound. Wales is next door and they too have made their contribution to what makes a Liverpudlian.

In addition, Liverpool has had a steady, if small, trickle of other nationalities who have come and settled in the city. Many were seamen and most settled near to the docks. Negroes from West Africa, working as firemen with the old Elder-Dempster line, Filipinos, Scandinavians. Men from all over the world. Plus, of

① O'Mara, P. 'Liverpool Slummy', The Bluecoat Press, Liverpool, 2009, p. 14.

② Lane, Tony 'Liverpool City of the Sea', Liverpool University Press, Liverpool, 1997, p. 16.

第一节　熔炉利物浦

美国总是以自己是不同种族和文化的熔炉而自居。在某种程度上确实如此，但还有一个事实：美国是一个种族关系紧张和自甘堕落的国家，并且存在种族隔离的情况。可是利物浦和利物浦人正如这座城市里人们最钟爱的本地菜“炖菜”一样：包容开放。炖菜是一种周围有什么就放什么的杂烩，主料来自英国、爱尔兰和威尔士，还放了很多来自非洲和亚洲的调料。

19 世纪 40 年代起，由于爱尔兰土豆饥荒，许多绝望的爱尔兰人开始陆续涌向利物浦，所以利物浦人的口音很大程度上受其影响。凯尔特人也把自己的基因融入到利物浦这个熔炉之中，他们的口音也为利物浦的语言注入了新元素。而与利物浦毗邻而居的威尔士，也为利物浦人的形成作出了他们的贡献。

另外，一直以来还有一些其他民族的少量外来者持续不断地迁徙到利物浦并在此定居。他们中的许多人都是水手并且大都在码头附近定居。来自西非的黑人、中国人、菲律宾人、斯堪的纳维亚人和来自其他国家的人一起在埃尔德登普斯特航运公司 (Elder-Dempster line) 做锅炉工。他们在码头附近还有市中心的一些地方定居，例如皮特街、费雷德里克街还有克利夫

course, the Chinese in and around an area close to the docks and the city centre-Pitt Street, Frederick Street and Cleveland Square. Many of these men with white wives and mixed race children.[①]

But the Chinese were said to choose their wives with care. Family was the foundation of their culture. A relationship was not something to be taken lightly. It was a commitment for life and children had to be cared for.

2.2 The Chinese are coming

By the end of the nineteenth century Liverpool was at its commercial peak. Second only to London in importance, it had produced more wealthy families in that century than any other city in Britain outside the capital. Its wealth was based totally on its position as a port. And amongst the wealthiest in the city were the Holt family.[②]

The Holt shipping line, or Blue Funnel as it had come to be known due to the colour of the exhaust stack of its ships, had steadily increased the number of Chinese it employed as the nineteenth century wore on. These numbers increased rapidly in the 1890s and it in this decade that we begin to see Liverpool's Anglo-Chinese community come into being. Very small at first, with fewer than 100 Chinese resident on Merseyside at the

① Craggs, S and Lynn, I Loh 'A History of Liverpool's Chinese Community', Merseyside Community Relations Council, Liverpool, 1985, pp.1 – 2.

② Lane, Tony 'Liverpool City of the Sea', Liverpool University Press, Liverpool, 1997, p. 14.

兰广场 (Pitt Street, Frederick Street and Cleveland Square)。他们中的许多人都娶了白人妻子，生育了混血的孩子。

据说中国人选择妻子非常谨慎。在中国的文化中家庭是一切的基础。两个人确定婚姻关系是很慎重的，因为这不仅是一生的承诺也是养育儿女的需要。

第二节　中国人来了

19 世纪晚期，利物浦的商业发展到了顶峰，其重要性仅次于伦敦。在 19 世纪，除了首都伦敦之外，利物浦的富裕家庭比其他任何一个城市都要多。利物浦的富裕完全取决于它的港口地位。而在利物浦市最富有的就是霍尔特家族。

由于船上烟囱的颜色，霍尔特航运公司或称为蓝烟囱航运公司开始为人所知。19 世纪，霍尔特航运公司雇佣的中国船员持续稳定增长。这一数量在 19 世纪 90 年代时激增，也是在那 10 年的时间里，我们可以看到利物浦华人社区渐渐形成。起初规模很小，20 世纪初时只有在默西赛德郡有不到 100 个华裔居民。10 年后，这一数量上升到 400 多人。规模虽然不大，但第一代英中混血子女已经开始在当地的学校读书。他们正在成为利物浦的一分子。

beginning of the twentieth century, ten years later the numbers had risen to over 400. Still not large but the first Anglo-Chinese children were attending the local schools. They were becoming part of Liverpool.①

The Chinese were coming but not everyone welcomed them. They may have been few in number but that was not how some locals saw the situation. The Chinese numbered tens of thousands they screamed. They were filthy, criminal. They were immoral. They were taking British jobs. They were taking the women.

How many Chinese were there? More than 30,000 said one article in the Liverpool Courier in 1906. To be precise, 30,568.② Not so, said the Head Constable, there were only 100 permanent residents and 300 temporary ones in the city.③Complete nonsense, said one Arthur Tutor at a meeting to protest at 'the Yellow Peril in Liverpool', there were at least three times that number. ④

Never mind the facts, yelled the agitators. The Chinese were diseased, criminal, paupers.⑤They were the lowest form of life on the planet. In the past five to ten years they had formed a colony

---

① Craggs, S and Lynn, I Loh 'A History of Liverpool's Chinese Community', Merseyside Community Relations Council, Liverpool, 1985, p. 4.

② 'Alien Trouble' in 'The Liverpool Courier', Friday, November 16th, 1906, Central Library, Liverpool, UK.

③ 'The Chinese Immigrants: Decision to Admit Them' in 'The Liverpool Courier', Thursday, November 29th, 1906, Central Library, Liverpool, UK.

④ 'International Octopus in Liverpool: The Chinese Importation – Indignant Protest' in 'The Liverpool Courier', Tuesday, December 4th, 1906, Central Library, Liverpool, UK.

⑤ 'Alien Trouble' in 'The Liverpool Courier', Friday, November 16th, 1906, Central Library, Liverpool, UK.

中国人来了，但并不是所有人都欢迎他们。虽然他们人数并不多，但当地人却不是这样认为的。他们叫嚷着这儿来了成千上万个中国人。他们污秽不堪，违法乱纪，道德败坏。他们不仅抢走了英国人的工作，还抢走了女人。

究竟当时有多少中国人呢？在 1906 年《利物浦信使报》的一篇文章中说到当时有超过 3 万个中国人，准确来说是 30568 人。然而警察局局长却说情况并非如此，当时市内只有 100 个永久华裔居民，300 个临时华裔居民。在“利物浦的黄祸”抗议会上，一位名叫亚瑟·图铎的先生反驳警察局局长说这是一派胡言，中国人的数量起码有 3 倍之多。

煽动者们喊道，不管事实如何，中国人有病，他们是罪犯，是乞丐，他们猪狗不如。在过去的 5 到 10 年里，中国人陆续在市内建立安置地并逐渐破坏和腐蚀英国人的道德。英国人和这帮中国佬没有任何共同之处。“他们是邪恶的人，他们的价值观和行为就是对我们道德规范的公然冒犯”，怒气冲冲的牧师威廉·卡特二世在一封给媒体的信中这样写道。这些话完全不像出自一个虔诚的基督徒之口。

in the city and were undermining and corrupting the morals of the English people.① The British had nothing in common with 'John Chinaman'. He was an evil creature whose values and behaviour were a '...deliberate affront to our moral code.' So thundered the Reverend William Carter junior in a not-very-Christian letter to the press.②

Perhaps the basic cause of all this was fear. Fear that the Chinese would out-compete the British worker. Fear that in what was regarded as a greatly overcrowded labour market, they would take the jobs of the British working class.③ It was obvious that they were willing to work harder than the British. They were willing to work all hours of the night and in the worst of conditions.④Most frightening of all, they would work for less, much less, than the British workers.⑤

The fear was greatest in the laundry trade where, it was claimed, hundreds of local Liverpool women had been put out of work by the Chinese.⑥ Women were not allowed to work at

① 'International Octopus in Liverpool: The Chinese Importation – Indignant Protest' in 'The Liverpool Courier', Tuesday, December 4th, 1906, Central Library, Liverpool, UK.

② Letter to the Editor from Reverend William Carter Junior 'Public Views on the Chinese Invasion' in 'The Liverpool Courier', Friday, December 7th, 1906, Central Library, Liverpool, UK.

③ 'Alien Trouble' in 'The Liverpool Courier', Friday, November 16th, 1906, Central Library, Liverpool, UK.

④ Interview with Arthur J. Tutor 'More Chinese in Liverpool: Increasing Indignation' in The Liverpool Courier', Friday, November 30th, 1906, Central Library, Liverpool, UK.

⑤ Letter to the Editor from Pro Patria in 'The Liverpool Courier', Wednesday, December 5th, 1906, Central Library, Liverpool, UK.

⑥ 'Liverpool's Yellow Peril: Chinese Capture of the Laundries – Displacement of British Labour' in 'The Liverpool Courier', Tuesday, December 11th, 1906, Central Library, Liverpool, UK.

也许发生这一切的根本原因就是恐惧。他们害怕中国人会取代英国工人，害怕中国人会在供大于求的劳动力市场上抢走英国工薪阶层的工作。因为很明显，中国人比英国人工作更加努力。即使身处恶劣的环境，他们也愿意通宵工作。而且最可怕的是，他们愿意接受比英国人少得多的工资。

洗衣业的人们最为恐惧。据称，有数百名利物浦女人因中国人而失业。因为当地女人不被允许在晚上工作，但中国男人却能够在晚上工作，而且他们也确实这样做了。面对这样的不公平竞争，当地家庭妇女选择支持英国洗衣店店主，她们认为应该把所有中国人从城市里赶出去。

night but Chinese men could and did work then. This was unfair competition and it was the duty of local housewives to support British laundry owners. The Chinese should all be cleared out of town.①

But how much of this anti-Chinese tirade was fact? That they worked hard was undeniable. But did they work for less than the locals? It seems not. The Chinese actually charged more than the locals and could do so because they produced better work. The British owned laundries had put themselves out of business by their own incompetence and poor quality work.②

So what? The answer was obvious, bellowed the China haters. Get rid of the Chinese and then all would be well again. But perhaps that was the real point at issue. The Chinese were just better at what they did. The British really could not compete. And that was just as true in the merchant marine where, as we shall see, a Chinese crew was what many British Captains preferred.

2.3 The Anglo-Chinese—a 'new race'

It was not only in the workplace that the British worker was finding it hard to compete with the Chinese. It was also becoming true in the marriage market. Chinese men were, as we have seen,

① Letter to the Editor 'Chinese Labour' in 'The Liverpool Courier', Thursday, November 29th, 1906, Central Library, Liverpool, UK.

② 'Liverpool's Yellow Peril: Chinese Capture of the Laundries – Displacement of British Labour' in 'The Liverpool Courier', Tuesday, December 11th, 1906, Central Library, Liverpool, UK.

但是这些反对中国人的长篇大论里有多少是事实呢？中国人工作努力是不可否认的，但他们挣得就比当地人少吗？事实似乎并不是这样。实际上因为中国人工作做得更好，所以他们比当地人要价更高。那些英国洗衣店店主是因为自身工作质量差，不能胜任工作而导致自己失业的。

那又怎样呢？办法很明显，仇视中国的当地人咆哮道：赶走那些中国人，一切都会再次好起来。但也许这正是问题的关键，中国人的工作就是做得好，英国人无法与其竞争。在商船上也是如此，正如我们所见，中国船员是许多英国船长的首选。

第三节　英籍华人——一个“新种族”

不仅是在就业市场上英国工人发现难以同中国人竞争，即使在婚配市场上也开始如此。正如我们所见，中国男人开始成为当地女孩的丈夫人选。这不可避免地引起了当地男性的嫉妒、激烈又恶毒的反响。当地男性呼吁应该保护姑娘们远离“黄祸”，女人，甚至是小孩走在他们所居住的街道也是不安全的。

starting to become the husband of choice for some local girls. Inevitably, the jealousy of the local males was aroused and the reaction was loud and vicious. Daughters should be protected from the 'Yellow Peril'.① It was unsafe for women or even children to walk the streets where they lived.②

But the protests were too late. Young women were making a choice and there were now small numbers of women around Pitt Street and elsewhere in the city with their '….half-caste Chinese children…'③ A so-called 'new race'④ who would have, said the jealous white males, '…all the vices found in human nature.'⑤

What was the real situation? According to Alderman Maxwell of Liverpool City Council, the number of resident Chinese in the city was only 224 and they were spread all over town. ⑥Mostly they were running laundries and employing British women to do the work. ⑦They were marrying local women and their children

① Letter to the Editor 'Chinese Labour' in 'The Liverpool Courier', Thursday, November 29th, 1906, Central Library, Liverpool, UK.

② Interview with Arthur J. Tutor 'More Chinese in Liverpool: Increasing Indignation' in 'The Liverpool Courier', Friday, November 30th, 1906, Central Library, Liverpool, UK.

③ Letter to the Editor from R. H. Foster in 'The Liverpool Courier', Saturday, December 8th, 1906, Central Library, Liverpool, UK.

④ 'International Octopus in Liverpool: The Chinese Importation – Indignant Protest' in 'The Liverpool Courier', Tuesday, December 4th, 1906, Central Library, Liverpool, UK.

⑤ Letter to the Editor from R. H. Foster in 'The Liverpool Courier', Saturday, December 8th, 1906, Central Library, Liverpool, UK.

⑥ 'Liverpool's Chinatown: Commission of Enquiry Appointed: Startling Statements – Government and the Aliens Act' in 'The Liverpool Courier', Thursday, December 13th, 1906, Central Library, Liverpool, UK.

⑦ 'Liverpool's Chinatown: The Alleged Overcrowding – Statement by the Medical Officer' in 'The Liverpool Courier', Friday December 7th, 1906, Liverpool Central Library, Liverpool, UK.

但抗议已经太迟了。年轻的姑娘们早已做出选择，那时在皮特街和市内其他地方已经有一小部分妇女生养了“中英混血的孩子”。这便是所谓的“新种族”，但心怀嫉妒的男性却称他们是“人性中所有罪恶的集合”。

真实的情况究竟是怎样的呢？根据利物浦市议会议员麦斯威尔所提供的信息，当时利物浦市内的华人居民只有 224 人，而且他们分散在全城各地，如西德比、托迪斯以及任何一个开洗衣店能够盈利的地方。他们大多数人都经营洗衣店并且雇佣英国女人为其工作。他们和当地女人结婚，随后他们的孩子开始在全城各地的学校上学。利物浦并没有被中国人占领，但英籍华人社区却开始在利物浦慢慢扎下了根，中国人也渐渐从和他们打过交道的人那里获得了尊重。

were starting to enter the schools all over the city – in West Derby, in Toxteth and everywhere that a profitable laundry business could be set up.① The city was not being over-run but the Anglo-Chinese community was taking root and the Chinese were gaining the respect of those who dealt with them.

The Chinese were law abiding. Not one case of theft or assault could be found in the records. They were said to give the police '… no trouble whatever.'② They made no claims for welfare and they were never found drunk and '…staggering around the pavements on a Saturday night, shouting and brawling, fighting the police, and knocking a defenceless woman about…'.③ They were, in many respects, ideal citizens and they were in the city to stay.

So, in these early years of the twentieth century we can see the pattern of Liverpool's Anglo-Chinese settlement. Chinese men, mostly seamen, come ashore. Those who stay settle down with local girls. Some set up businesses close to the docks. In the area around Pitt Street to serve Chinese mariners temporarily on shore. Others enter the laundry trade. They operate as family businesses with their white wives and mixed race children. These businesses steadily spread throughout the city. This spread means that there is

① 'Chinatown in Liverpool: An Unofficial Chinese Consul – Little Aliens and Home Life' No. 4 by a Special Correspondent in 'The Liverpool Courier', Monday December 17th, 1906, Liverpool Central Library, Liverpool, UK.

② Letter to the Editor from Fair play to all in 'The Liverpool Courier', Friday December 7th, 1906, Liverpool Central Library, Liverpool, UK.

③ Letter to the Editor from Chin Chin in 'The Liverpool Courier', Saturday December 8th, 1906, Liverpool Central Library, Liverpool, UK.

中国人遵纪守法，没有任何一项偷窃或是斗殴的犯罪记录。据统计，他们没给警察“添一丁点儿麻烦”，他们从不要求福利，不会醉酒生事，也不会“在周六晚上的人行道上喝得酩酊大醉，又喊又叫又袭警，将路过的手无寸铁的女人打倒在地”。在很多方面，中国人是这座城市里的理想公民。

因此，在20世纪前期我们就可以看出利物浦华人定居的模式。中国男人大多是船员，下船后同当地的姑娘结婚安顿下来。一些人在码头附近做起了生意，在皮特街周边为临时上岸驻足的海员提供服务。另一些人则是带着自己的白人妻子和混血孩子干起了家庭作坊式的洗衣店。他们的生意稳定地在市内扩展，顺利的扩展意味着华人社区形成的道路几乎没有阻碍。而这些英籍华人家庭中长大的孩子对自己父亲的文化背景和语言知之甚少，他们作为利物浦人长大成人，通常与白人社区的人结婚。

little in the way of a Chinese ghetto. The children of these Anglo-Chinese families grow up knowing little of their father's culture and nothing of his language. They grow up as Liverpudlians and often marry into the white community.

But what of the children of the men who married local girls but continued to work as merchant seamen? The Chinese seaman was paid less, significantly less, than his white counterpart. But he was, as the Courier admitted, not likely to spend his money on alcohol, the curse of the British seaman. He provided well for his family. But his children too grew up as Liverpudlians. Their father was away up to nine months of every year. What chance did they have to learn his language or his culture? As with the laundry children, the influences around them were Liverpool working class. Even for the children who grew up in Chinatown, the person who influenced them most was their mother. Their Liverpool Irish 'Mam'. And the language spoken in the streets and the school playgrounds where they mixed with other white and mixed race children was Liverpool's own version of the English language. The dialect and accent that would identify them very firmly as Scousers.

而那些继续从事船员工作并同当地女子结婚的中国男人的孩子是什么样呢？中国船员的工资很低，比和他们做同样工作的白人的工资低得多。但就连《利物浦信使报》都承认，中国男人不太可能和英国船员一样，把钱花在酒精上。他们生活节俭，却为家庭提供了良好的生活条件，他们的孩子也是作为利物浦人而长大成人。这些孩子的父亲们每年要离家 9 个月，他们哪有什么机会去了解父辈的语言和文化呢？至于洗衣店里长大的孩子，他们身受利物浦工人阶层的影响。即使是唐人街长大的孩子，影响他们最深的人也是他们的母亲，他们的爱尔兰裔利物浦“妈妈”。在街道上和学校操场上混杂着白人孩子和混血孩子，他们所讲的语言也是利物浦版本的英语。受周围这些方言和口音的影响，这些混血孩子们坚定地认同自己就是利物浦人。

03

Chapter 3. World War I and its aftermath

第三章　第一次世界大战及其余波

The second decade of the twentieth century was to see the death of millions and the collapse of Empires. The destruction of a world order that had seemed fixed and firm just a few short years before.

The first Empire to fall was on the other side of the world to Liverpool. The Qing dynasty in China had been slowly falling apart for decades. But when it finally collapsed in 1911 it still seemed to take the Chinese and the Europeans living in China by surprise. The next forty years would see China ravaged by struggles between Various armed forces. It would see a Japanese invasion that would lead to the deaths of millions and match in every way the barbarity of the Nazis in Europe. It would see a brutal civil war between the Nationalist Party, nominal rulers of China under Chiang Kai-shek, and the Communists led by Mao Zedong. The incentive for people to leave China had never been greater.

In Europe the First World War would destroy the Romanov Empire in Russia, the Austro-Hungarian Empire in Central Europe, the German Empire throughout the world and would shake the British Empire to its core. Tens of millions would die and the Europe that would emerge from this holocaust would never be the same.

The impact of the War on Liverpool was immense. Not only were thousands of men killed in the trenches on the Western Front but thousands more died at sea. The shipping companies had to

20 世纪的第二个十年见证了数以百万计生命的消亡和帝国的覆灭。几年前似乎还稳定坚固的世界秩序瞬间就被打乱了。

第一个倒下的帝国便是位于世界另一端、与利物浦相对的中国清王朝。虽然在数十年的时间里清王朝缓慢地分崩离析，但 1911 年清王朝最终覆灭的消息还是使中国人和居住在中国的欧洲人大为震惊。在接下来的近 40 年里，中国大地在为未来寻求光明与正义的历程中饱受了各种战争之苦。而日本人的侵略更是导致了数百万人的死亡，其残暴程度与欧洲的纳粹相比，在各个方面，有过之而无不及。此外，在中国，蒋介石带领的国民党和由毛泽东领导的共产党之间爆发了一场惨烈的内战。连年的战争迫使人们强烈地想逃离这个国度。

在欧洲，第一次世界大战摧毁了俄罗斯的罗曼诺夫帝国、中欧的奥匈帝国、遍及世界的德意志帝国，并且也动摇了大英帝国的根基。数以千万的人死于战争，而经历过这场浩劫的欧洲也永远不会和之前一样了。

“一战”对利物浦的影响是巨大的。不仅数以千计的人死在西线的战壕里，更有成千上万的人死在海上。航运公司不得不找人代替那些死于战争的人或是被皇家海军征召的经验丰富

replace the men who were being killed and the experienced seamen who had been taken into the Royal Navy. Britain turned to the men of its Empire – Indians and Africans. But it also recruited the men of its unofficial Empire – China. It recruited them both for its merchant fleet and for the Western Front in France.①

The Army recruited the big men of Shandong Province in Northern China as labourers on the Western Front. Here they dug the trenches, carried the munitions and buried the dead. Many were killed and buried in France where some of those who survived stayed and settled. The curious can see the graves of three of those who died in the Chinese section of Liverpool's Anfield cemetery.

The shipping companies also turned to the Chinese, as they had in the Napoleonic Wars, Up to six thousand were recruited into the merchant fleet. Many of these men were based in Liverpool with around 1500 of them in the city at any one time.② And as it was to be in the next global conflict, Liverpool was Britain's most important port as the UK grew to rely ever more on American manufactured munitions and equipment. After 1917 it was American manpower that was coming ashore as the city became the disembarkation point for the American troops flooding into Europe.

With so many Chinese in the city, the Liverpool Anglo-Chinese community received a huge boost. Indeed, many

① Wood, F. 'No Dogs and Not Many Chinese: Treaty Port life in China 1843 – 1943', John Murray, London, 1998, p. 52.

② Evans, Bob 'Mersey Mariners', Countyvise, Birkenhead, 1997, p. 260.

的海员。英国开始征召其殖民地的人——包括印度人和非洲人，除此以外，还从中国征召人手。这些人有的被召去商船船队，有的被送往法国的西方战线做劳工。

军队征召了中国北方的山东大汉作为西线的劳工。他们在这里挖战壕、搬军需、埋尸体。许多人死在法国并埋葬于此，幸存的人留在这里并安顿下来。有兴趣的人可以在利物浦的安菲尔德公墓的中国区域看到有这样三个中国人的坟墓。

正如拿破仑战争时期一样，除了军队，航运公司也把目光转向了中国人。商船船队招募的中国人人数达到了6000人。他们中的许多人都居住在利物浦，而且无论何时城中也有1500人左右。随着英国越来越依赖美国生产的军需和设备，利物浦也成了英国最重要的港口，这就引发了接下来的冲突。1917年，当这座城市成为美国部队进入欧洲的登陆点后，美国劳工也涌入到了这座城市。

有了这么多中国人在城中，利物浦华人社区得到了迅速发展。事实上，许多华裔利物浦人将华人社区的发展归功于那些在“一战”中敢于驾驶英国船只面对北大西洋上游弋的U型潜艇的中国海员们。

Liverpudlians who have Chinese ancestry owe it to a merchant seaman who braved the U-boats sailing the North Atlantic on a British ship during that War.

3.1 A quiet and civil man

The Empire may have needed the skill and bravery of the Chinese mariner in its struggle against the U-boat but, once again, as had happened less than ten years before, the Chinese in Liverpool were under attack from some of the locals.

This time it was the British seamen's union that was making all the anti-Chinese noise. The head of the National Union of Sailors and Firemen, Havelock-Wilson, had been complaining about Chinese men on British ships since before the War. By 1911 he was claiming that there were 45,000 Chinese and Indians on British ships. A figure almost ten times the actual number.[①] The real complaint was, as it had been with the laundrymen, their supposed cheapness and willingness to work in almost any conditions. A willingness driven by the poverty and growing chaos back in China.

That the Chinese seaman was cheap was true. He was paid around 40% of his British counterpart. But it was not true that, as was claimed, he was useless as a seaman. He was much less likely to desert his ship than the British seaman almost 25,000 of who

① MSS 175/3/16/2 'Chinese Invasion of Great Britain: A National Danger', National Seamen's and Firemen's Union, Modern Records Centre, University of Warwick, UK.

第一节　中国船员，安静而文明

大英帝国可能需要技术娴熟而勇敢的中国海员与 U 型潜艇做斗争，但是正如不到 10 年前所发生的那样，利物浦的中国人再一次受到了当地人的攻击。

这一次是英国海员工会的人发出了反对中国人的抗议。在“一战”爆发之前，英国水手及机工工会主席哈夫洛克 - 威尔逊就已经开始控诉中国人在英国船上工作的事了。1911 年，他声称在英国船上工作的中国人和印度人有 45000 名。这一数字大概是真实人数的 10 倍。但实际上，控诉的真相和之前的洗衣业一样，是中国工人的廉价和在任何情况下都能投入工作的意志，一种被贫穷和中国愈演愈烈的混乱而驱使着的意志。

中国海员的廉价是事实，与相同职位的英国海员相比，中国海员大概只有其 40% 的工资。但中国海员适任能力差的这一说法却与事实相差甚远。仅 1908 年一年，就有大概 25000 名英国海员弃船，而中国海员比英国海员弃船的概率要小得多。在如此鲜明的对比之下，一些英国船长更喜欢中国船员并且要

deserted in 1908 alone.[①] So good in comparison was the Chinese mariner that some British Captains preferred Chinese crews and requested them. Typical of the views of so many British merchant marine Captains was that of one Captain Froggart of the India Monarch. In his opinion the Chinese seaman '...compared to the European is infinitely the better man. He is steady, willing and a good worker and also a quiet and civil man.'[②] A better worker and a better man.

As the war in Europe dragged on the shortage of manpower became ever more evident as casualties mounted in France. In 1916 the British Army suffered 60,000 dead and wounded on the first day of the Battle of the Somme.[③] But this reality had scant impact on the campaign being mounted against the Chinese by National Sailors and Firemen's Union. As men were being slaughtered on the Somme, he wrote to the King complaining that the Chinese were taking the jobs of British sailors. The British sailors who by 1917 made up half the membership of the American Seaman's Union and 75 percent of that Union's membership in the Atlantic Trade.[④]

But once the War ended, the situation changed and, as was to happen after World War II, moves to get rid of the Chinese

① Lane, Tony 'Liverpool City of the Sea', Liverpool University Press, Liverpool, 1997, p. 75.

② Quoted in pamphlet in MSS 175/3/16/2 'Chinese Invasion of Great Britain: A National Danger', National Seamen's and Firemen's Union, Modern Records Centre, University of Warwick, UK

③ Middlebrook, M. 'The First Day of the Somme', Allen Lane The Penguin Press, London, UK, 1971, pp. 263-271.

④ Lane, Tony 'Liverpool City of the Sea', Liverpool University Press, Liverpool, 1997, p. 75.

求招聘他们。“印度君主”号船长弗洛加特是许多英国商船船长的典型代表。在他的观点里，中国海员“比起欧洲人要好得多。中国人沉稳、安静又文明，并且乐于付出，是很好的海员”。中国人不仅是出色的海员，也是优秀的人种。

随着战争在欧洲战场的持续，在法国战场的伤亡人数不断增加，人力资源的短缺也变得越来越明显。1916 年索姆河战役打响的第一天，英国军队的伤亡人数就达到了 6 万人。但这一事实并没有阻止由英国水手及机工工会领导的反对中国人的运动。当战士们在索姆河被屠杀时，哈夫洛克却写信向国王控诉中国人抢走了英国海员的工作。而 1917 年，美国海员工会中有一半是英国海员，并且 75% 的工会船员都工作在大西洋航线上。

“一战”结束后情况发生了变化，正如第二次世界大战结束后所发生的一样，清除中国人的行动最终还是开始了。通过不断的施压，最后哈夫洛克－威尔逊施加在船东身上的压力开始奏效了。尽管之前许多英国船长会优先选择这些工作勤奋、头脑清醒且不酗酒的中国海员，但现在这些中国船员发现自己已很难找到工作了。随着时间的流逝，他们积欠房东的房租也

began. At the end of the conflict the pressure that had been exerted on the shipowners by Havelock-Wilson began to bear fruit. The diligent and sober Chinese mariner, despite being preferred by so many British Captains, found he was no longer wanted. Men found themselves unable to get work. Debts to the boarding house keepers continued to mount as the months passed by. And while Holt continued to use Chinese crews, other companies who had been glad of their industry and low cost during the War bowed to the pressure brought on them by the Union of Sailors and Firemen. The result was hundreds of men found themselves stranded on shore.

As they would do after World War Two, the British authorities considered deporting the Chinese who had so recently risked their lives for the country. They were told, as they would be little more than twenty-five years later, that deportation would be unlikely to be legally enforceable. Threats to the Chinese Government were considered – the men would never again obtain employment with a British company if they did not leave. There would be race riots.[①] But they could not leave. Havelock-Wilson and the British seamen's union had seen to that the situation dragged on with some of the Chinese taking almost two years to get a ship out of the UK. Many found themselves effectively working for nothing on their voyage back home. So great had their debts to the boarding house keepers become that they had to hand over all their advances of pay to clear their debts.

① Wong, M. L. 'Chinese Liverpudlians: a History of the Chinese Community in Liverpool', Liver Press, Birkenhead, 1989, pp. 82-83.

越来越多。虽然霍尔特公司继续雇佣中国海员，但那些在战争期间对自己的经营和低廉的成本感到满意的其他航运公司，现在也都向英国水手及机工工会所施加的压力屈服了。这一局面导致数以百计的中国船员滞留在岸，无法上船工作。

正如英国政府在“二战”后的做法一样，此时他们想要遣返这些不久前还在为这个国家出生入死的中国人。他们被告知，正如25年后那样，遣返中国人很可能无法合法实施。于是他们考虑威胁中国政府：如果滞留在英国的中国人无法遣返，英国公司将永远不会雇佣他们，并且有可能会发生严重的排华事件。但中国海员无法离开，哈夫洛克－威尔逊和英国海员公会目睹了遣返工作的进展缓慢，一些中国海员花费了近两年时间才搭上离开英国的船舶。许多人在回家的旅途中发现自己的辛苦劳作换来的却是一无所获。他们积欠房东太多房租，不得不将自己预支的工资用来缴清欠款。

In a tragic rehearsal of what was to happen again at the end of the Second World War, marriages and long-term relationships were shattered as men were forced to leave. Men who made their lives in the city, had wives and families in the town, were caught up in the stampede to get rid of the Chinese.① Children were left fatherless and women plunged into poverty. Maria Lin Wong in her book Chinese Liverpudlians quotes a leader in the Daily Telegraph deploring the fact that the wives of the men made to leave the UK had been abandoned. No recognition of the harsh reality of the manner in which the men had been forced to leave. The leader does mention the women 'taken to a hostile land'.② The wives of Chinese who had chosen to go with their men to China rather than be separated from them. This too was to happen again after World War II.

3.2 Social and financial chaos

The aftermath of War was that after the short-lived post war boom the social and financial chaos caused by the war began to take its toll. The world map was redrawn in the Peace Conference at Versailles. In Europe new countries came into being, borders moved, Russia dissolved into civil war. In Germany the bloody

① Letter from H.M Inspector, Office of the Superintending Aliens Officer, Liverpool, June 20th, 1919; File HO 139/147, Home Office, National Archives, Kew, UK.

② Wong, M.L. 'Chinese Liverpudlians: a History of the Chinese Community in Liverpool', Liver Press, Birkenhead, 1989, p.82.

在第二次世界大战结束后，这些悲剧又会重演，而这一次就像是提前彩排。当中国海员被迫离开时，他们的婚姻以及长期的感情关系也随之瓦解。在城里谋生或是有妻室的男人都被卷入了这场清除中国人的狂潮中。他们的孩子失去了父亲，妻子陷入贫困。玛利亚·林·王在《中国裔利物浦人：利物浦华人社区的历史》这本书中引用了《每日电讯报》的一篇社论，揭露了当时被迫离开英国的中国海员的妻子被抛弃的事实，却没有提及这些男人是以何种方式被逼离开的残酷真相。但在社论中却提到了女人们“被带到了一片充满敌意的土地”，这些中国劳工的妻子宁愿选择和自己的丈夫一起回到中国也不愿和他们分开。而这种情况在第二次世界大战后会再度重演。

第二节　社会与经济混乱

战后迎来了短暂的繁荣，随之而来的是战争的苦果，由于战争造成的社会和经济混乱开始肆虐。在凡尔赛和平会议上世界被重新划分。在欧洲，新的国家开始形成，边界改变，俄国陷入内战。在德国，血腥的内部冲突和恶性通货膨胀使得纳粹开始掌权。而在英国，爱尔兰在内战中分裂，英国的失业率不断攀升。

civil conflict and hyperinflation that was to bring the Nazis to power began. Closer to home, Ireland tore itself apart in its own civil war, Britain saw unemployment move steadily upwards.

For Chinese the Peace Conference was a frustrating and humiliating experience. They found that the principles of equality espoused by the American President Woodrow Wilson did not apply to non-whites. There was to be no statement that even hinted at racial equality. The white man did decide to give Japan the areas in China that had formerly been controlled by Germany. That these areas were not in the gift of the Europeans and Americans was, apparently, an irrelevance. The Chinese were not, of course, consulted.

For China this was as harsh a blow as could be imagined. Tens of thousands of their young men had worked with the Allies. Many had died. But this was to count for nothing. Their land was to be parcelled out as those Allies saw fit. It has long been the role of Chinese intellectuals to act as the conscience of the nation. It was expected that they sacrifice themselves, if necessary, in the cause of justice and right, on May 4th 1919 Chinese students demonstrated against the Allies decision.①

The so-called the May Fourth Movement , as it came to be known in China, has become part of the history of the struggle for people's rights in that country. And it did have some effect. The Japanese did not get the land in China that they had taken from

① Spence, J.D. 'The Search for Modern China', W.W. Norton and Company, London, 1999, pp. 299 – 308.

对于中国来说，和平会议却是一次令其备受侮辱的经历。他们发现美国总统伍德罗·威尔逊所谓的平等原则并不适用于非白种人，根本没有关于种族平等的声明，甚至连一点暗示也没有。和平会议中决定把中国先前归德国管辖的区域分给日本。这些原本属于中国的区域，不是欧洲的，也不是美国的，在赠予日本之前，却一点都没有征求中国的意见。

可以想象这对中国是多么沉重的打击。成千上万的年轻人曾为协约国工作，许多人还为此丧命，到头来这些却毫无价值。协约国把他们的国土分成块，看到哪块合适就割走。而长久以来，中国的知识分子一直扮演着国家的良知这一角色，甚至他们愿意为了正义和权利而牺牲自己的生命。在 1919 年 5 月 4 日这一天，中国学生示威反对协约国的决定。

五四运动在中国尽人皆知，它已经成为了人民为权利而反抗的标志性历史运动，而且还取得了一定的效果。战后，日本并没有得到战时从德国手中抢走的中国土地。因此日本心怀怨恨，这也促使日本军方取得了国内政权并决定使用武力拿回本该分给他们的东西。很快，他们侵略了满洲，利用中国最后一

the Germans during the War. The Japanese retreated into a bitter resentment that helped hand power to the military and determined them to take what they had not been given. They would soon invade Manchuria, set up their own puppet government under the last Emperor of China and move to take over the whole country.

Europe was torn and bleeding but would slowly recover some order and limited affluence in most parts of the continent before tearing itself apart again no more than twenty years later. The North of England would not share in the recovery that came to the South of the country and Liverpool, dependant on shipping and a key port for the China trade, would be particularly hard hit. China was sliding rapidly into blood-soaked fratricidal misery. As we will see, this would impact on Liverpool's Anglo-Chinese community for decades to come.

3.3 The Great Depression

By 1926 the British economy was in trouble. A long and fruitless strike by the coal miners and an equally fruitless General Strike in the same year were symptoms of the economic ills facing the country. Britain relied on trade. It was almost a century since she had been able to produce enough food to feed her population. She relied on exports to pay for her food and raw material imports. And since the end of the nineteenth century she had had to face two great industrial rivals – the USA and Germany. She was no longer

任皇帝建立起傀儡政权并且要占领整个中国。

战后的欧洲四分五裂、流血不止，不过欧洲大陆的大部分地区慢慢地恢复了秩序并得到有限的发展，而这仅仅维持了不到20年，欧洲再一次四分五裂。依靠航运业和与中国的贸易，英国南部和利物浦得到了一定的恢复，然而，英格兰北部地区在遭遇战争的严重打击后，并没有像南方一样恢复过来。战后中国仍处于军阀混战之中。如我们所见，这些将会在接下来的几十年里都影响着利物浦的华人社区。

第三节　经济大萧条

到1926年时，英国的经济陷入困境。一场由矿工发起的漫长而无果的罢工加上同年爆发的一场同样毫无结果的大罢工体现了这个国家所面临的经济弊病。英国依赖贸易业，其粮食生产无法自给自足，近一百年来，一直依靠出口所得支付其粮食和原材料进口的花费。自从19世纪末，英国就面对着两大工业劲敌——美国和德国。英国再也不是世界工厂了，其制成品出口早已不能支付其支出账单。英国开始利用金融方面的专业知识转向对外投资。但是在战争结束后，为了偿还在美国购

the Workshop of the World. Her manufactured exports had not been able to pay her bills for a long time. She relied on her foreign investments and financial expertise to do that. But by the end of the War there was little left of these investments. They had been sold to pay for the war materials she had to buy from the USA.

Now Britain was also faced by what was, in part, a self-imposed problem. The Allies had been warned of the economic consequences of the punishment they intended to impose on a defeated Germany. Maynard Keynes, the most famous economist of the twentieth century, had told them that the result would be disastrous for trade between nations. [①]Nevertheless, they went ahead. At the Versailles Peace Conference the Allies decided that Germany must pay for the damage caused by the War. This meant that she had to export to earn the money to pay, but much of the countries earnings would be taken in reparations to the victors. As a result she had little left to pay for imports. As Keynes had forecast, the pattern of international trade was severely disrupted. Britain had been a major exporter to pre-War Germany, but Germany could no longer buy British goods. As a consequence, Britain's earnings were dramatically cut and the countries that owed her money could not pay as trade faded away. Britain still had to pay her debts to the USA. The Great Depression was standing in the wings waiting to make its entrance.

As the economic situation worsened through the 1920s,

① Keynes, J. M. 'The Economic Consequences of the Peace', Harcourt Brace, New York, 1920.

买的军需物资，这些投资已经所剩无几。

现在英国所面临的困难在一定程度上也是自找的。协约国曾被警告过，对战败国德国的惩罚将会带来的经济后果。20世纪最著名的经济学家梅纳德·凯恩斯曾说过，战后对德国的经济惩罚将会给国家间贸易带来灾难性的后果。尽管如此，在凡尔赛和平会议上，协约国依然判决德国必须支付战争给其他国家所造成的损失。这意味着德国不得不通过出口的方式换取外汇以支付赔偿。将国家的大部分生产所得用于向胜利国缴纳赔款后，德国几乎没有能力再支付进口的费用。正如凯恩斯的预测，国际贸易的模式被严重打乱。英国一直是战前德国的最大出口国，但现在德国已经没有能力继续购买英国的产品。结果，英国的收入急剧下降，当贸易逐渐停滞，其他国家无法偿还英国的债务，英国又要偿还美国的欠债时，大萧条时代如期而至。

随着20世纪20年代经济状况的恶化，政府开始限制进口，以此保护本国产业，而这进一步加剧了国际贸易的萎缩。航运

governments reacted by imposing restrictions on imports to protect home industry. International trade shrank and shrank. The shipping industry was hard hit and Liverpool was severely affected. This meant that the literal and figurative lifeblood of its Anglo-Chinese community rapidly drained away. The Chinese men who had come in the early years of the century were ageing and as they passed away they were not replaced. Less ships meant fewer Chinese seamen coming to the city and fewer coming ashore to settle.

The Anglo-Chinese community had always been spread throughout the city. The laundry trade had seen to that. The Chinatown of Pitt Street and the surrounding area was where the old men met on a Sunday. It was where the Chinese seamen stayed in the boarding houses built to accommodate them. It was where they ate the food that was familiar to them. A study by Liverpool University in 1931 showed that there were now no more than 500 adult Chinese men remained in Liverpool. Mostly laundrymen married to local women, they were spread throughout the city.[①] Those out of work had been deported and the Depression was ensuring that the numbers of Chinese mariners was shrinking. The economic problems facing the world and the 1914 British Nationality and Status of Aliens had practically stopped all Chinese settlement in the city.[②] As the old Chinese men died and their children and grandchildren married into the surrounding white

① 'Chinatown' in Post and Mercury, April 25th, 1934, Liverpool Central Library, Liverpool, UK.

② Jones, D. 'The Chinese in Britain – Origins and Development of a Community' in 'New Community' Vol vii, no.3, 1979.

业遭受严重打击后，利物浦也深受影响。这也意味着利物浦华人社区的发展遇到了严重的阻碍。在世纪初来到英国的中国人正渐渐老去，而当他们去世后却没有人能顶替他们的空缺。船只越来越少意味着来利物浦的中国船员越来越少，而上岸定居的也越来越少。

利物浦华人社区一直遍布全城，从洗衣业便可见一斑。老人们周日在皮特街的唐人街和附近区域聚会。这里有为中国的海员们而建的寄宿屋，也有他们熟悉的饭菜。1931 年，利物浦大学的一项研究显示，当时只有不到 500 名成年中国人仍在利物浦。大部分洗衣店的男人都娶了当地的女人，他们为了照顾生意，分散在全城。那些失业的人被遣返回国，而经济大萧条导致中国海员的数量不断减少。世界所面临的经济问题和《1914 年英国国籍和外国人身份法案》基本阻止了中国人到利物浦定居。当老一辈的中国人去世，他们的子辈孙辈由于婚姻而融入了附近的白人社区，唐人街便慢慢消失了。1934 年时，议会决定重新开发这一区域。皮特街的街道将拓宽至 60 英尺，而这一区域内逐渐减少的利物浦华人社区“将会找到一个新的归宿”。

community, Chinatown faded away. By 1934 the Council had decided to redevelop the area. Pitt Street would be widened to 60 feet and the dwindling Anglo-Chines community in the area '... would have to find a new home.'①

The plans came to nothing. In a city dependant on the sea and the trade it brought, the Council lacked the finance. By 1938 so small had the community become that in April of that year the Chinese Christian church in the Edge Hill district of the city held its last service.② There were simply not enough Chinese left in the Liverpool to form a viable congregation.

Then the Second World War broke out.

① 'Chinatown Doomed' in 'Post and Mercury', November 19th, 1934, Liverpool Central Library, Liverpool, UK.

② Article in 'Liverpool Echo'. April 12th, 1938, No author cited. Liverpool Central Library, Liverpool, UK.

结果由于海上贸易的减少，利物浦市议会缺乏资金，这一计划完全失败了。到 1938 年时，社区的规模已经非常小了，同年 4 月在知山区的华人基督教会举办了最后一次礼拜，因为留在利物浦的中国人已经少得无法维持教会活动了。

随后第二次世界大战爆发了。

04

Chapter 4. The War begins

第四章　战争开始了

The Chinese Wars

For the Chinese in Liverpool the War did not start in September 1939. It had been going on for many years. Supporters of China's Nationalist Government in Liverpool, mainly Cantonese from Hong Kong and the surrounding Province of Guangdong, had long been sending money to China to give what help they could in its struggle with Japan. Their headquarters, initially in Pitt Street but now to be seen in Nelson Street, became the hub of its efforts as Japan became ever more aggressive in its campaign to colonise China.

Japan had been expanding its influence in Northeast area of China since its victory over Russia in 1905. From then on it had steadily increased its control of this area, one fifth of the Chinese land mass. In 1931 the Japanese Kwantung Army seized Mukden and quickly took control of the rest of Northeast area. Then, on 28th January 1932, it attacked the Chinese sector of Shanghai. China was at war with Japan.[①]

The Cantonese Nineteenth Route Army fought them from street to street and house to house. To their shame, the British running the so-called International Settlement allowed the Japanese to unload tanks, artillery, armoured cars and munitions. The Nationalist sent in their best German-trained troops but, outgunned, the Chinese lost more than 10,000 dead and missing before being

① Fenby, J. 'Generalissimo Chiang Kai-shek and the China He Lost', The Free Press, London, 2003, p. 209.

中国的战争

对于身在利物浦的中国人来说，第二次世界大战并非开始于 1939 年 9 月，而是已经持续了多年。在利物浦的国民政府的支持者主要是广东人，他们来自香港以及广东周边的省份，一直寄钱回国为抗日战争提供帮助。他们的总部一开始位于皮特街，后来搬至纳尔逊街。随着日本侵略中国的军事行动越来越激烈，这里已成为一个抗日斗争的枢纽。

日本自从 1905 年打败俄国后，就开始扩大其对中国东北的影响。从那时起，日本逐步加强对东北的控制，东北占中国大陆面积的五分之一。1931 年，日本关东军占领了奉天并且迅速控制了东北。随后在 1932 年 1 月 28 日，日本袭击上海的非租界区。中国与日本展开了激战。

主要由广东人组成的国民革命军第十九路军同日本人一条街一条街、挨家挨户地战斗。而英国应该感到羞耻的是，他们竟然允许日本人在其管辖下的所谓的公共租界里卸下大炮、坦克装甲车和军需品。国民党派出由德国训练的精锐军队但仍旧不敌，在被迫撤退之前已经有超过一万人死亡或失踪。

forced to retreat.

On March 1st 1934 the Japanese had the last Emperor of China declared Emperor of their puppet state of Manchukuo,① the former Chinese Provinces of Northeast of China. Pu Yi Aisin-Gioro had been a child when the Empire collapsed in 1911 and had been a virtual prisoner ever since.

Now the Nationalists in Liverpool were sending their money home not just for the fight against the Japanese. By the time of the first Japanese attack on Shanghai the civil war with the Communists had been underway for 5 years. And the deep divide and mutual hatred of the Nationalists and Communists was to have enormous impact on Liverpool and its Anglo-Chinese community. This was to be evident both during the War that was now certain to come and after it as men were forced out of the city.

The animosity was not just due to conflicting ideologies. It was also, to a significant extent, a split between Cantonese and Shanghainese. Overseas Chinese communities, it seemed, tended to divide up into district association, clans and sub-districts.② Liverpool's Chinese community added to this naturally explosive mix of differences in language and, even more divisive, conflicting political beliefs-Nationalists versus Communists. Not only did this tear the community asunder, it turned family members against each

---

① Aisin-Gioro Pu Yi 'From Emperor to Citizen: the Autobiography of Aisin Gioro Pu Yi' Vol. 2, translated by W.J.F. Jenner, Foreign Languages Press, Peking, 1979, p. 276.

② Lee, M. T. 'Growing Up in Chinatown: the Life and Work of Edwar Lee' Fong Brothers Printing Inc, USA, 1987, p. 46.

1934 年 3 月 1 日，中国最后一任皇帝在日本控制下的傀儡政府伪满洲国称帝，其前身是中国的满洲省。1911 年，当大清帝国倾覆时爱新觉罗·溥仪还是一个孩子，自此之后他实际成为了一名囚犯。

而当时身在利物浦的国民党党员向国内寄钱不仅仅是为了抗击日本，因为在日本袭击上海前，国民党与共产党之间的内战已经进行 5 年了。国共两党间的巨大分歧对利物浦及其华人社区也有着巨大的影响。这在即将到来的战争中还有在战后人们被赶出英国时更为明显。

这种仇恨并非仅仅来源于意识形态的冲突，在很大程度上也取决于广东人和上海人的分歧。海外华人社区似乎趋于分成区协会、宗族和小区协会。利物浦华人社区也自然而然地产生了这种爆炸式的碰撞，除了语言方面的不同，更多的碰撞来源于政治信仰的分歧和冲突，即国民党与共产党之间的对抗。这不但使得社区分崩离析，还使家庭成员之间反目成仇。

other.

The Chinese Nationalist Party had been founded by Sun Yat-sen. Canton, as it had been known to Western traders for centuries, was re-named Guangzhou by the Communists when the civil war ended in 1949. Shanghai was where the Chinese Communist Party had been founded. It had come into being in that city's French Concession. A part of the city run by the French and known for its notoriously corrupt and inept administration. Nevertheless, Shanghai was the Chinese city most open to Western influence and, like Liverpool, a city with a reputation for radicalism. As we shall see, it was the Shanghai men in Liverpool during the War who were to be regarded as the most militant and who would be the focus of the shipping lines efforts to get rid of those they and the Government labelled as 'troublemakers' and 'left wing agitators'.

The bitterness between the two language groups also owed much to Chiang Kai-Shek and his determination to destroy the influence of the Communists in China's greatest city. Following the entry of the Nationalist Army into Shanghai in 1927, Chiang and his hoodlum allies, the Green Gang, had massacred hundreds of members of the Communist Party and their supporters.[①] And Chiang's connection with the head of the Gang, Big Eared Du, was rumoured to go back a long way. The bloodbath forced the Communists out of the city and into the countryside where they

① Li, L.T. 'Madam Chiang Kai-shek' Grove Press, New York, 2006, p. 75.

中国国民党是由一位名为孙中山的人创立。几个世纪以来，广州（Canton）一直为西方商人所熟知，当1949年内战结束后，共产党将其更名为广州（Guangzhou）。中国共产党成立于上海市内的法租界。法租界是在上海市内一部分由法国管理的区域，以其臭名昭著的腐败以及管理无能而为人所知。尽管如此，上海仍是中国对西方最开放而且受其影响很大的城市，就像利物浦一样，也是一座有着激进主义名声的城市。正如我们所见，在战争时期身在利物浦的上海人被认为是最不安分的群体，并且也是航运公司的关注重点，他们以及那些被政府打上“闹事者”和“左翼煽动者”标签的人都是被清除的对象。

这两个语言群体间的痛苦很大程度上是蒋介石造成的，因为他铁了心要摧毁共产党在中国最重要的城市中的影响力。1927年，随着国民党军队进入上海，蒋介石和他的流氓盟友青帮屠杀了数百名共产党员及其支持者。而且据说蒋介石与青帮头目杜月笙交情已久。这样的屠杀逼得共产党不得不从城市转向了农村，从而与国民党政府打响了持久的游击战。尽管存在日本人对国民政府的威胁，这场持久战一开始，共产党胜利的可能性看似微乎其微。

began their long guerrilla war against the Nationalist Government. A guerrilla war that, initially, was far from successful despite the pressure being exerted on the Nationalist Government by the Japanese.

By 1934 the Japanese military had taken control of most of Northern China. Despite this Chiang and the Nationalists were still focusing their military efforts on defeating the Communists whose main base was in Jiangxi Province in the southeast of the country. With the help of his German advisers, Chiang developed a strategy that gradually strangled the effectiveness of the base. Three thousand concrete blockhouses were built around it. Linked by roads and bridges to facilitate the easy movement of troops and munitions, these served to cut off supplies to the Communists and eventually forced them into undertaking the fabled Long March. It was a desperate attempt by the Communists to escape and survive. But few did survive. Of the up to 100,000 who set off on this about 7767 mile trek, only ten per cent reached Yan'an. The Communists were trapped in their new base in remote Shanxi Province, in the far North-West of China next to Inner Mongolia.①

Still the war with Japan went on with the next major incident affecting the British and again centred on Shanghai. In mid-August 1937 Chiang ordered his best troops, the 87th and 88th divisions to fighting back Japanese positions around Shanghai. At least 800,000 troops were to be engaged in this second battle for

① Spence, J.D. 'The Search for Modern China', W.W. Norton and Company, London, 1999, pp. 397 – 403.

到 1934 年，日本军方已经控制了中国北方大部分地区。尽管如此，蒋介石和国民党还是把主要军事力量都集中在打击共产党上，共产党的主要根据地位于中国东南部的江西省。蒋介石在德国顾问的帮助下，制定了一个逐渐遏制根据地的有效战略。他们在共产党根据地周围建立了 3000 个混凝土碉堡，与道路、桥梁相连接，这不仅有助于灵活便捷地运输军队和军需，同时也切断了共产党的补给。共产党被迫选择长征，10 万人长途跋涉约 7767 英里，造成了大量伤亡，最后只有大约百分之十的人抵达延安 。共产党到了新的根据地，其位于中国西北部偏远的陕西省，紧邻内蒙古。

中国与日本的战争仍在继续，而下一个影响英国的重大事件再一次发生在上海。1937 年 8 月中旬，蒋介石命令其精锐部队，第 87 师和第 88 师主动反击日本在上海的阵地。在上海的第二场战争中至少有 80 万名士兵参战，随着日本对这座城市的不断轰炸和炮击，伤亡不断增加，残酷的肉搏战再一次上演。最终，中国人不敌日本人的火力优势，在 11 月上旬，蒋

Shanghai with the carnage growing as the Japanese bombed and shelled the city. Once again vicious hand-to-hand fighting raged in the Chinese sector. But history repeated itself as superior firepower wore down the Chinese. Eventually, in early November, Chiang ordered a retreat. The Chinese had lost, by some estimates 300,000 men. The Japanese perhaps 70,000 of their troops.[①]

Refugees poured into the largely British run International Settlement of Shanghai by the tens of thousands as the Japanese pursued the retreating Chinese Army. Reaching Nanjing the Japanese perpetrated one of the worst atrocities in modern history. Three hundred thousand Chinese civilians were killed as the Army rampaged through the city. Men, women and children were buried alive, women raped before being shot and civilians used for sword practice by Japanese officers.[②]

The impact of all this on Liverpool's Anglo-Chinese community requires little imagination. For those with family in Ningbo, Shanghai and Hong Kong news came with the men sailing to and fro on the Blue Funnel boats. Frightening as it was, at least they had some idea of what was happening. They could send money. They could send letters. But for those born outside of these areas their fears for those of their family back in that country were made worse by the difficulties of communication as more and more of China fell into Japanese hands.

---

① Fenby, J. 'Modern China: the Fall and Rise of a Great Power 1850 to the Present', HarperCollins, New York, 2008, pp. 278-280.

② Ibidem pp. 280 – 281.

介石下令撤退。据估计中国有 30 万人员伤亡，而日本军队大概有 7 万人员伤亡。

日军在追击撤退的中国军队时，数以万计的难民涌入大部分由英国管辖的上海公共租界。南京沦陷后，日军实施了近代历史上最惨无人道的暴行。日军在城内施暴，屠杀了 30 万中国百姓。男人、女人和孩子被活埋，女人被强暴后再被枪杀，日本军官甚至用中国平民来练习军刀。

可想而知这些事对利物浦华人社区的影响。对于那些在宁波、上海和香港还有家人的人来说，他们尚且能从乘坐蓝烟囱轮船往来的人那里打听到一些关于家乡的消息。尽管令人惊恐，但起码能对家乡发生的事情有些了解。他们可以寄钱，可以送信。但对于那些不是在这几个地区出生的人们，由于很难得到家人的消息，他们对于在国内的家人的担心，随着中国土地一步步沦入日本人之手，变得更加强烈了。

However, the main concern of those in the community who were not born in China was the worsening situation in Europe. The Nazi terror had been growing in Germany with Jews, faced with no other sanctuary taking refuge in Shanghai.① Nazis aggression in Europe was increasing. The German Army had marched into Austria in March 1938. And, as the decade began to draw to its close, the German Chancellor Adolph Hitler was demanding that the Czech Republic cede to Germany the territory on its western boarders inhabited by the so-called Sudeten Germans. Browbeaten by Hitler and with no support from Britain or France, the Czechs handed over the territory in September 1938. The British Prime Minister, Chamberlain might cry 'Peace in our time' as this was done but there were those who now knew that war was now inevitable.

By September 1939 the Nationalist Government in China had retreated to the remote inland city of Chonqing in Sichuan Province in the southwest of China bordering Tibet. Now the Japanese controlled China's most productive Provinces and Chonqing's only links with the outside were by air or via the famed Burma Road.② The cities effectively controlled by western countries, particularly Hong Kong, Shanghai and Ningbo, were amongst the very few places in the country that still had access to the outside world.

① Wasserstein, B 'Secret War in Shanghai: Treachery, Subversion and Collaboration in the Second World War', Profile Books, London, 1998, p. 140.

② Spence, J.D. 'The Search for Modern China', W.W. Norton and Company, London, 1999, pp. 425-426.

然而，在华人社区内，对于那些出生在英国的华人，他们担心的主要是不断恶化的欧洲局势。身在德国的犹太人不像上海的难民一样能够找到避难所，他们对于纳粹的恐惧不断加深。纳粹在欧洲的侵略行径愈演愈烈。1938年3月，德国军队入侵奥地利。20世纪30年代末，德国元首阿道夫·希特勒要求捷克共和国将其西部边界的领土让与德国，理由是那里居住着所谓的苏台德德国人。在希特勒的威逼之下，又没有英国与法国的支持，1938年9月，捷克共和国将那块领土割让给了德国。当这件事结束时，英国首相张伯伦还在呼喊着“这是属于我们这个时代的和平”，但是已经有很多人意识到这场战争已经不可避免。

1939年9月，日本已经控制了中国最为富饶的省份，中国国民党撤退到了中国西南部与西藏相邻的偏远内陆城市——重庆市，而重庆与外界仅有的联系只能通过航空运输或是著名的滇缅公路。在受西方国家控制的中国城市中，香港、上海和宁波是国内仅有的几个还能与外界有联系的城市。这些地方仍然是利物浦华人社区打听消息的渠道，而消息仍然使人们担忧。这也激化了持不同政治主张群体之间的紧张局面。战争的乌云越来越阴暗了。

They were still the channel by which Liverpool's Anglo-Chinese community got its news. News that continued to worry its people. That continued to increase the tension between its different groups with their conflicting political sympathies. And the clouds of war were getting darker.

Hitler's armies invaded Poland and on September 3rd 1939 Britain declared war on Germany. The Second World War had begun and soon the world's first truly global conflict would engulf the planet. As in the First World War, Chinese seamen in their thousands would serve in the British merchant marine and Liverpool's Anglo-Chinese community would see its last great flowering.

希特勒的军队入侵波兰,1939年9月3日,英国对德国宣战。第二次世界大战爆发，世界真正意义上的第一次全球冲突很快吞没了整个星球。正如第一次世界大战一样，数以千计的中国海员将会受雇为英国商船工作，而利物浦华人社区也将会迎来最后一次繁荣。

05

Chapter 5. The War at sea

第五章　海上战争

After the rapid collapse of Poland, each side considered its next moves. Hitler horrified his General Staff by insisting on an invasion of France.① Plans had to be made and this took time. The Allies considered a range of options – but did nothing. The 'Phoney War' had begun.

That was true for the army and for the civilian population but it was far from true for the Royal Navy and for the merchant marine. Within less than a month of the start of the War the British had lost the aircraft carrier HMS Courageous and the battleship HMS Royal Oak to U-boat attacks. In the South Atlantic the German pocket battleship Admiral Graf Spee sank nine merchant ships in the first three months of the war.② Amongst the crews of these ships were a number of Chinese seamen and they were to figure in a dramatic rescue early the following year.

On February 16th 1940 a German vessel, the Altmark, was carrying British merchant navy prisoners back from the South Atlantic – men whose ships had been sunk by the Graf Spee. Chased by British destroyers she took refuge in a Norwegian jord. Churchill, then First Lord of the Admiralty, ordered Captain Vian of HMS Cossack to enter the jord, board the Altmark and rescue the prisoners. In the subsequent celebrations back in the UK no mention was made of the significant number of Chinese mariners. It seemed that although the Chinese seamen were well and truly involved in the War and exposed to the same dangers as any other

① Liddell Hart, B. 'History of the Second World War', Pan Books, London, 1973, p. 39.

② Ibidem pp. 386-387.

波兰迅速沦陷后，各方都在考虑下一步行动。希特勒执意要进攻法国，其总参谋部因此惊恐万分，进攻必须要制订计划，而且需要时间。盟军方面考虑了一系列方案，但最终什么也没做。对于陆军和平民来说，“静坐战”打响了。

但对于皇家海军和商船队来说，情况却完全不同。在战争开始还不到一个月的时间里，英国已经因为U型潜艇的袭击损失了“勇敢”号航空母舰和“皇家橡树”号战列舰。在战争的前三个月，德国的“斯佩”号袖珍战列舰在南大西洋击沉了9艘商船。在这些商船船员中就有许多中国海员，他们在来年年初参加了一次惊心动魄的营救行动。

1940年2月16号，德国“阿尔特马克”号补给舰从大西洋返航，船上拘押着英国商船海员俘虏，他们的船被“斯佩”号击沉。由于被英国驱逐舰追捕，“阿尔特马克”号逃入挪威峡湾。那时身为英国海军大臣的丘吉尔命令“哥萨克”号的维安上校进入峡湾，登上“阿尔特马克”号并救出了被俘船员。而在随后英国的庆祝活动中，却没有提到众多参与施救的中国海员。尽管中国海员确实参与到战争中，也曾跟其他海员面对着一样的风险，但至少在官方消息中没有中国海员的身影。

sailor, officially at least, they were invisible.

But how could thousands of men be invisible? From 1939 to the end of the war Holt and Anglo-Saxon Petroleum, better known to the public as Shell, ran their Chinese Seamen's Reserve Pools out of Liverpool.① This meant there were 20,000 Chinese seamen based in the port with thousands on shore at any given time.

The men were from many parts of China but predominantly they came from just three locations. As Fred Bishop had seen, many were from Hong Kong and Shanghai. These were usually sailing on Holt ships with the company taking most of its men from Shanghai at this time.② A fact that, as we shall see, would have a huge impact on Liverpool's Anglo-Chinese community during the War and its fate after the conflict had ended.

The Anglo-Saxon company took its men predominantly from Singapore. Both companies signed the men on two-year contracts with the right to discharge in the port at which they signed on. For most of them this meant back in Asia and Holt in particular were to take great advantage of this term in the men's contracts when the end of the War eventually came.

As had been the case since the Chinese had first been employed on British vessels, they came cheap. Very cheap. At this time the basic pay for a British seaman under National Maritime

① Whitingham-Jones, B. 'China Fights in Britain: A Factual Survey of a Fascinating Colony in Our Midst', Hurricane, W.H. Allen and Company, London, 1944, p. 8.

② Falkus, M. 'The Blue Funnel Line Legend: a History of the Ocean Steamship Company 1865-1973', MacMillan, London, 1990.

但是数以千计的人怎么会毫无踪影呢？从 1939 年到战争结束时，霍尔特和盎格鲁 – 撒克逊石油公司，即公众熟知的壳牌石油公司，他们在利物浦城外经营着中国海员后备队。这意味着无论何时都有约 2 万名中国海员储备在各港口，数千名海员在岸上生活。

这些人来自中国各地，但主要来自三个地区。正如弗雷德·毕晓普曾见到的那样，他们中的许多人来自香港和上海。因为那时候公司招聘的大部分人都来自上海，所以通常在霍尔特船上航行的就是这些人。正如我们所见，这些事实不仅会对战时的利物浦华人社区有着巨大的影响，同时还会影响到他们在战争结束后的命运。

而盎格鲁 – 撒克逊石油公司主要从新加坡招工。这两个公司都和其员工签订了两年的合同并且有权在雇佣他们的港口解雇他们。对于他们中的大多数人来说，这意味着在战争结束后，霍尔特公司将充分利用合同中的这项条款解雇他们，他们还要回到亚洲。

英国商船一开始雇佣中国人时，工资就非常低廉。那时一名为国家海事委员会效力的英国海员的基本工资每月大概是 12 英镑 12 先令 6 便士，约合 12.6 英镑，而霍尔特付给中国海员的基本工资大概是 4 英镑 13 先令 9 便士，约合 4.7 英镑。由于在盎格鲁 – 撒克逊石油公司的油轮上工作的人面临的危险更大，所以新加坡海员的工资大概在 5 英镑 15 先令，约合 5.75

Board rates was £12.12.6 a month-approximately £12.60. Holt's basic pay for a Chinese rating was £4.13.9 – approximately £4.70. For the greater danger of working on Anglo-Saxon's oil tankers, the men from Singapore were paid £5.15.0 – around £5.75.① This in conditions that were so poor they were said to be '...not really suitable for white crews.'②

For the Liverpool women married to Chinese seamen the low pay meant constant worry about how to make ends meet as prices rose steadily as the war went on. Now this was to be overwhelmed by the fear that the ships their men were on would not return.

5.1 The Phoney War ends

The headlines in the British newspapers of April 9th 1940 screamed out that on the previous day British and French naval forces had entered Norwegian waters and laid minefields there. Churchill had decided to take action to try to disrupt any ships trading with Germany. But the radio that morning gave out even more dramatic news – German forces were landing on the Norwegian coast and were invading Denmark. British forces reached Norway within the week but found themselves unable to overcome the Germans.③ On June 7th they were evacuated along

① 'Note on Negotiations with Representatives of the Chinese Government', March, 1942, File MT 9/3743 Ministry of War Transport, National Archives, Kew, UK.

② Ibidem.

③ Fraser, D. 'And We Shall Shock Them: The British Army in the Second World War', Cassell and Company, London, 2002, p. 52.

英镑。待遇如此微薄，因此他们说不适合白人海员。

对于嫁给中国海员的利物浦女人来说，随着战争继续，物价持续上涨，低收入意味着要不断担忧怎样维持收支平衡。现在这种担忧已经被另一种恐惧替代，因为载着她们丈夫的船只可能永远都回不来了。

第一节　静坐战结束了

1940年4月9日英国各报纸的头条刊登：在前一天英法两国海军进入挪威水域并在那里布好了雷区。丘吉尔决定采取行动阻断一切和德国进行贸易的船只。但是那天上午广播马上就播出了更戏剧性的消息——德军于挪威海岸登陆并开始入侵丹麦。之后，英军在当周内赶到了挪威但却不敌德军。6月7日，他们同挪威国王和政府官员一起撤退。相比于整个战局，这时的挪威事件不过是一段小插曲而已。

with the Norwegian King and the country's Government. However, by this time, Norway was very much a sideshow.

On May 10th 1940 Hitler's forces broke through the defences of the Allies and were soon in France. By 13th they had crossed the river Meuse at Sedan, the site of the German defeat of the French in 1870. Within days reached the Channel coast and the Allied armies were cut off in Belgium. On 26th the British Cabinet authorised the withdrawal of British troops from Dunkirk. By June 2nd they had got 224,000 of their men off the beaches plus 95,000 other Allied troops, mainly French. The French Government accepted Hitler's surrender terms on 22nd June.[①]

Now the British were alone on their island and completely dependant on the merchant fleet to be able to fight on. For it was that fleet which had to bring in the supplies she needed to continue the war. The authorities well knew that this was going to be difficult in the extreme and that the German Kriegsmarine would do everything it could to cut Britain's supply lines.

With the surrender of France the U-boat threat had grown. Now they had additional bases in Brest, Lorient and La Pallice. All 700 kilometres closer to the Atlantic than their bases in the North Sea. This meant they could attack convoys further to the west and spend much longer hunting in the sea-lanes. The impact of this was soon to be felt. Fifty-eight ships were sunk in June 1940 and an average of 250,000 tons of British merchant shipping was to go to

① Ibidem, p. 79.

1940 年 5 月 10 日，希特勒的军队突破盟军防线并迅速进入法国。13 日，他们已跨过色当的默兹河，这也是 1870 年德国击败法国的地点。然后在不到几天的时间内，他们到达了英吉利海峡沿岸，而此时盟军军队却被困于比利时。26 日，英国内阁授权英国军队从敦刻尔克撤退。到 6 月 2 日，已有 22.4 万名英国人另加 9.5 万名盟军士兵撤离，其中大多是法国人。6 月 22 日，法国政府投降，并接受了希特勒提出的投降条件。

此时孤军奋战的英国，只能完全依靠商船队带来的补给才能战斗下去。英国当局非常清楚这将是极其困难的，因为纳粹德国海军将会采取一切办法来切断他们的补给线。

随着法国的投降，德国 U 型潜艇的威胁进一步增加。现在德国海军在布雷斯特、洛里昂和拉帕利斯有了新的基地，比起其在北海的基地离大西洋近了整整 700 公里。这意味着德国海军可以袭击更靠西面的船队而且可以在海上进行远距离猎杀。影响很快显现出来，1940 年 6 月有 58 艘船被击沉，而在接下来的每个月便会有平均 25 万吨位的英国商船沉入海底。

the bottom of the ocean in each of the following months.①

The fears of the Liverpool women married to merchant seamen, Chinese or British, were now becoming reality. By September 1940 around 100 Chinese seamen and many hundreds of British seamen had died. Hitler had ordered that the tankers must be attacked first. They carried the oil without which Britain could not fight. They, as we have seen, were often manned by the Chinese. But, unlike the family of a British seaman, when a Chinese seaman died, his wife and family in Liverpool faced immediate poverty. Not only had they lost their partner and the income that he earned. They were now to discover that the compensation they would receive would be far less than the family of a British seaman.②

As 1940 wore on the casualties in the merchant fleet mounted. Sixty-three merchant vessels, a total of 350,000 tons of shipping, were sunk in October alone. Convoy SC7 with a naval escort of four ships lost almost two thirds of its number. A few days later HX79 lost 25% of its numbers despite a heavy escort including two of the scarce destroyers and four corvettes. Corvettes were now being used in increasing numbers because of the acute shortage of the better-armed and more suitable destroyers. The number of widows in Liverpool was increasing by the week.

Although the pressure from the U-boats eased as the winter

① Liddell Hart, B. 'History of the Second World War', Pan Books, London, 1973, p. 390.

② Lane, Tony 'Sons of Empire', Manchester University Press, Manchester and New York, 1990, p. 162.

那些嫁给中国或是英国商船海员的利物浦女人的恐惧正在成为现实。到 1940 年 9 月，已经大约有 100 名中国海员和好几百名英国海员死去。希特勒下令优先袭击油轮，因为英国没有油就无法战斗。正如我们之前提到的，这些船上通常工作着中国海员。但不同于英国海员家庭，当一名中国海员去世时，他在利物浦的妻子和家庭马上就面临着贫困的威胁。她们所失去的不仅仅是丈夫和他们的收入，还发现即使是抚恤金，也远远低于英国海员。

1940 年，英国商船船队的损失不断增加。仅在 10 月就有 63 艘商船被击沉，总吨位达 35 万吨。SC7 船队加上为其护航的四艘军舰几乎损失了总船队数量的三分之二。几天后，HX79 船队在两艘稀有的驱逐舰和四艘轻巡洋舰的重重护卫下仍然损失了 25% 的船只。由于装备精良、适合护航的驱逐舰严重短缺，被迫大量使用轻巡洋舰。因此利物浦的遗孀人数每周都在持续增加。

虽然冬季的到来使大西洋的海况非常恶劣，来自 U 型潜艇的威胁得以缓解，但猎杀仍在继续。德国此时在挪威和法国之间投入使用福克沃尔夫远程轰炸机，仅在 11 月就击沉了

made conditions in the Atlantic difficult for them, the slaughter went on. Long-range Focke-Wulf bombers operating from Norway and France entered the fray. In November alone they sank eighteen ships. The German Kriegsmarine's surface vessels also began to make inroads into the British merchant fleet and the Chinese were in the thick of it. One Chinese mariner was able to write his eyewitness account of an attack by the Admiral Scheer on November 5th 1940 on convoy HX-84 out of Halifax, Nova Scotia. Sailing on a tanker, the seaman witnessed the armed merchant cruiser the Jervis Bay, the only escort for the 37-ship convoy, attacking the Scheer. Blown out of the water by the cruiser's more powerful armament, the Jervis Bay's sacrifice limited the losses in the convoy to five ships.① But many convoys did not escape so lightly. On February 12th 1941 the German cruiser Admiral Hipper sank seven out of nineteen ships in the unescorted convoy SLS64. More men died-both British and Chinese.

And the situation was to get much worse over the coming months.

5.2 Der Rudeln–the wolf packs

The British had gone back to the convoy system early in the conflict. It was a technique that had served them well against the U-boats in the First World War and it was quickly put into

① Lo, K.H.C. 'Forgotten Wave', Padiham Advertiser Ltd., Padiham, 1947, pp. 9 –15.

8 艘船。纳粹德国水面舰艇也开始袭击英国商船队，而中国人正处于这场生死搏斗中。一位中国海员写下他的目击记录，在 1940 年 11 月 5 日，驶出新斯科舍省哈利法克斯港的 HX84 船队遭到了“舍尔海军上将”号的袭击。正在油轮上的海员目睹了他们 37 艘船中唯一的护航舰——武装商船“杰维斯湾”号，抗击“舍尔海军上将”号。“杰维斯湾”号在海面被巡洋舰强大的火力炸飞，它的牺牲帮助其船队把损失限定在了 5 艘船。而其他许多护航船队就没那么轻易逃脱了。1941 年 2 月 12 日，德国巡洋舰“希佩尔海军上将”号击沉了 SLS64 船队 19 艘船中的 7 艘船。许多英国人和中国人在海上死去。

在接下来的几个月里，情况变得更糟糕了。

第二节　狼群战术

在战争初期，英国再次采用船队护航的方法，这项措施在第一次世界大战对抗 U 型潜艇时发挥了很好的作用。他们很清楚，无论护航船队规模大与小，德军在广阔的海洋中很难发现他们。遗憾的是，德军破解了英国海军 3 号密码，于是他

effect again. They knew that the Germans had problems spotting a convoy in the vastness of the ocean whatever the size of that convoy. Sadly, the Germans had broken the British Naval Cypher 3 and were able to estimate where and when convoys could be expected. In early 1941 they renewed the U-boat assault on the British merchant fleet and this time the threat was increased by the introduction of 'wolf pack' tactics. Admiral Donitz, the commander of the U-boat fleet, had first used these in October 1940 and he steadily refined them over the following months.

Sinking rose to new heights. By June 1941 over 30,000 tons of merchant shipping a month was being sunk.[①] Vessels were sliding beneath the waves faster than the shipyards could replace them. Although the situation improved as the year wore on and Canada became involved in convoy escort duties, merchant navy casualties continued. Between April and December 1941, 328 ships were sunk and on them were many Chinese mariners.

All this time Chinese seamen were earning a fraction of the pay of their British counterparts. For those with no family back on Merseyside, they were fighting and dying in a war that did not affect their homeland. Worse still, Chinese mariners with relatives back in China found the news from home was getting worse by the week.

5.3 The situation for the Chinese

With the fall of France the new Vichy Government had cut

① Liddell Hart, B. 'History of the Second World War', Pan Books, London, 1973, p. 396.

们能估计出护航船队出现的地点和时间。在 1941 年早期，他们更新了 U 型潜艇并袭击了英国商船队，随着“狼群战术”的实施，威胁进一步增加了。在 1940 年 10 月，德国海军及 U 型潜艇队的总司令邓尼茨第一次使用这个战术，并在接下来的几个月里不断将其完善。

沉船数量达到了新高。到 1941 年 6 月，德国在一个月内击沉了超过 3 万吨的商船，船舶沉入海底的速度比船厂再造的速度还快。随着时间的推移以及加拿大参与到护航船队之中，情况有所好转，但商船海员的死伤人数仍在增加。在 1941 年 4 月到 12 月之间，328 艘船被击沉，这些船上有许多中国海员。

一直以来，中国海员只能得到与其同等职位的英国海员工资的一小部分。对于那些没有在默西赛德郡建立家庭的人，虽然他们在海上冒着生命危险在战斗，但没有人会关心、牵挂他们。更糟糕的是，中国船员自己还牵挂着国内的亲戚，而国内传来的坏消息一个比一个糟糕。

第三节　中国人的处境

随着法国的沦陷，新维希政府切断了其越南殖民地至中国西南部云南的铁路线。英国也封闭了从缅甸至中国西南的公路。

the rail link from their colony of Vietnam to Yunnan in south–west China. Britain also closed the road from Burma to southwest China. China's military supply route was severed.

The struggle between the Communists and the Nationalists was continuing despite the Japanese invasion. One set of incidents in particular heightened the tensions between the Cantonese and the Shanghai men in Liverpool who by 1941 were split into two opposing trade unions. One of those unions, made up mainly of Cantonese, was linked to the Nationalist. The other was Communist and dominated by Shanghai and Singaporean seamen. The split was now complete and total and would be reflected in what happened to the men and to their families a few short years later.

The incidents that ratcheted up the tensions and widened the split concerned the 100,000 strong Communist Fourth Army. This had strong links to Shanghai and was made up not only of peasants but also workers, students and intellectuals from that city. Based on the Lower Yangtze, it was seen as a particular threat by Chiang Kai-Shek who had made that area his power base before the war with the Japanese. In autumn 1940 the Nationalists attempted to force the Fourth Army northwards but were decisively defeated in the battle that ensued. Chiang issued an ultimatum for the Fourth Army to go north but when it began to do so on the 4th of January 1941, Nationalist patrols opened fire. Under artillery and air attack and confronted with a much larger Nationalist force, the Communists lost up to 10,000 dead. Women were raped, prisoners

中国军方的补给路线被切断了。

尽管日本正在侵略中国，但中国共产党与国民党之间的斗争仍在继续。1941 年起，身在利物浦的广东人和上海人分为两个对立的工会，一系列特殊事件加剧了紧张的局势。其中一个工会主要由广东人组成，与国民党有联系。另外一个工会主要由上海和新加坡的海员组成，与共产党有联系。现在两个工会已经完全决裂，而且将会在接下来的几年内一直影响着他们及其家庭。

使得紧张局势加剧、分歧扩大的事件与共产党管辖下的、拥有 10 万部众的新四军有关。新四军由农民、工人、学生和知识分子组成，与上海有着紧密的联系。他们的根据地位于长江中下游，而这对蒋介石来说是一个极大的威胁，因为早在抗日战争前他就将这片区域作为自己的权力基地。1940 年秋天，国民党试图用武力强迫新四军北撤，但在占有优势的局面下却彻底战败。[①] 蒋介石向新四军下了最后通牒命其北撤，当新四军开始北上时，国民党驻扎部队却在 1941 年 1 月 4 日向新四军开火。面对着国民党的大炮、空袭以及众多的兵力，共产党损失了近 1 万人。女人被强暴，俘虏被枪毙或者活埋。不可避免地，从上海驶向利物浦的船只带来了这些消息。

① 即黄桥战役。—— 译者注

shot or buried alive.[①] Ships sailing from Shanghai to Liverpool would inevitably bring the news with them.

By now it was not just the Chinese civil war that was putting pressure on the men in Liverpool and on their families. The war with Japan was exerting ever-greater stress on them.

For those men from Ningbo sailing for Blue Funnel there now came terrible news that made them desperately worried about their relatives and friends in that city. Japanese planes had dropped fleas carrying plague germs. Tested on Chinese prisoners in the Japanese biological warfare facility in Manchuria, the plague germs now caused an outbreak of the dreaded Black Death in the city.[②] Ningbo, so close to Shanghai, was the hometown of many of the men based in Liverpool. Men were the husbands and partners of Liverpool women and would soon become the fathers of Liverpool children.

The Chinese were now exposed to the physical danger and mental stress of two wars. A European war that meant they were hunted by the wolf packs at sea and on shore, as we shall see, they were subject to the intense bombing of the Luftwaffe as it tried to destroy Liverpool's docks. They were getting dreadful news from the war in China that was multiplying that stress and building an ever-greater gulf between the Cantonese and the men from Shanghai. It was not surprising that many of the men wanted to go

① Fenby, J. 'Generalissimo Chiang Kai-shek and the China He Lost', The Free Press, London, 2003, pp. 363 – 365.

② Ibidem p. 359.

至此，不仅中国内战给生活在利物浦的中国人还有他们的家庭带来了巨大的压力，与日本的战争更是给他们施加了前所未有的压力。

对于来自宁波为蓝烟囱公司工作的人们，现在打听到了更可怕的消息，使他们极其担心仍在城内的亲朋好友。日本 731 部队在满洲用中国俘虏做活体实验制造出鼠疫菌，然后用飞机在宁波投下染有鼠疫菌的跳蚤，使城内爆发了致命的黑死病。宁波紧邻上海，是许多身在利物浦华人的家乡。他们也是利物浦女人的丈夫和伴侣，和即将出生的利物浦孩子的父亲。

利物浦的中国人现在正处于两场战争的生命危险和精神压力之下。欧洲战争意味着他们在海上被狼群战术所猎杀，而在岸上，正如我们所见，德国空军试图摧毁利物浦码头时他们又成为了密集轰炸的目标。中国战场传来的可怕消息更增加了他们的压力，并在广东人和上海人之间造成了更大的分歧。在工作中，相对于英国海员，中国海员的生命贱如蝼蚁，不被珍视，在这种情况下，许多人想要回国的想法也就不足为奇了。

back, particularly when it seemed that their lives were valued at so much less than the life of a British seaman.

By now British seamen were getting danger money for sailing in those vital convoys. Initially £5 per month, this was soon to be increased to £10. An almost doubling of their pay. In sad contrast, payment to the Chinese was at the discretion of the shipowners, was uncertain and highly variable.①

The issue of the War Risk Bonus became ever more contentious as the War dragged on and merchant navy casualties mounted. But this was not the only grievance of the Chinese. Unfair treatment and physical violence leading, in some cases, to the death of Chinese seamen was causing growing bitterness.

It seemed that it was becoming the norm to solve disputes with the Chinese by force. A dispute that began in September 1940 was brought to an end in April 1941 with men being imprisoned and then deported. The value afforded a Chinese life was nowhere better illustrated than in the case of the master of the tanker Silverash. During a dispute in New York he shot and killed one of his Chinese crew. In the subsequent trail he was found to have '... no case to answer...'②

So bad did the situation become that Anglo-Saxon Petroleum had to issue an official notice to its ships officers that the company would not stand for '...any physical violence against Chinese

① Lane, Tony 'Sons of Empire', Manchester University Press, Manchester and New York, 1990, p. 162.

② Ibidem, p.156.

现在这些至关重要的船队中的英国海员除了工资，还得到了战时津贴。一开始每个月 5 英镑，很快涨到 10 英镑，收入几乎翻了一倍。相比之下，中国人的工资是由船东决定的，不稳定且多变。

随着战争的继续和商船海员死伤人数不断增加，战时津贴的争议越来越多。但中国海员的不满并不只是这一点，不公平待遇和肢体暴力时而导致中国海员死亡，使得中国海员的不满持续增加。

后来似乎以武力来解决与中国人的争端已经成为了一种惯例。一场开始于 1940 年 9 月的争端在 1941 年 4 月以将罪犯监禁后并驱逐出境而结束。一名中国人生命的价值在这个案件里得到了极致的诠释，在纽约，“银灰”号油轮的船长跟一名中国船员在争执中开枪射杀了他，而在接下来的庭讯中却发现自己根本“无须答辩”。

由于情况十分恶劣，盎格鲁 – 撒克逊石油公司不得不向其高级船员发布了一份官方通知，公司不会容忍“对中国船员的任何暴力行为”。然而，问题并没有得到解决。1942 年时，中国驻英大使顾维钧博士曾写信给英国战时运输大臣莱塞斯勋爵，说明关于英国船上的争执导致中国海员死亡的情况。

ratings...'① However, the problem did not go away. In 1942 we find the Chinese Ambassador to the United Kingdom, Dr. Wellington Koo, writing to Lord Leathers, the British Minister for War Transport, about the disputes on British ships that were resulting in the deaths of Chinese seamen.②

The threat of death at sea, the threat of death from the Luftwaffe on land and violence on board ship. Little wonder that there was developing a sense of mutual distrust and enmity between the Chinese, the shipowners and the British Government. In particular, the Ministry of War Transport and the Foreign Office.

The Chinese were being seen as a constant source of aggravation as they protested at the situation in which they found themselves. In return, the Chinese themselves became deeply resentful of the treatment they were receiving. Treatment that violated their sense of how employers should behave. Loyalty was supposed to be rewarded with care and respect. Not with force. This was not happening and as a result they felt a '...collective sense of grievance...which was unabated for the duration of the War.'③

Then the Japanese invaded Hong Kong and Singapore and moved in to take over Shanghai. The Chinese mariners could no longer go home. They were stuck in Britain on Chinese pay.

① Letter from H.W Rowbottom of Anglo-Saxon Petroleum to N.A. Guttery, Ministry of War Transport, 18th March, 1942; File MT 9/3743, Ministry of War Transport, 1942, National Archives, Kew, UK.

② Letter from Dr. Wellington Koo, Chinese Ambassador to the UK to Lord Leathers, Minister of War Transport, 1st April, 1942; File MT 9/3743, Ministry of War Transport, 1942, National Archives, Kew, UK.

③ Lane, Tony 'Sons of Empire', Manchester University Press, Manchester and New York, 1990, p. 163.

在海上面临着死亡，在陆地上面临着德国空军的威胁，在船上面临着暴力。所以中国人与船东以及英国政府之间的互不信任和相互敌意也就不足为奇了，尤其是对英国战时运输部与外交部来说。

当中国人抗议自己所身处的环境时，他们却被视为事态不断恶化的根源。中国海员不满于自己的待遇，可是船东对于他们的抗议没有作出任何积极的反应。他们的忠诚应得到的是关心和尊重，而不是暴力。然而他们一直没有等到，因此在战争期间他们“普遍感到不满，并且这种不满一直持续着”。

不久之后，日本侵占了香港和新加坡，随后入侵并接管了上海。中国海员再也不能回家了，他们拿着微薄的收入有家难回。

06

Chapter 6. Strike!

第六章　罢工!

6.1 The Japanese attack

At 7:55 am on December 7th 1941, Japanese aircraft attacked the American fleet at Pearl Harbour. By the time the second wave of Japanese planes flew back to their carriers, almost 2500 Americans were dead, four American battleships had been sunk and another four had been badly damaged.① But critically for the Japanese the American carriers had been at sea during the attack. The same carriers that were to inflict such a crushing defeat on the Japanese Imperial Navy at Midway just six months later.

For Shanghai the war with Japan started one hour after the beginning of the attack on Pearl Harbour. At 4 am local time the Japanese boarded the two remaining non-Japanese war ships still on the Whangpoa. The USS Wake and HMS Peterel were overcome in minutes.②

On 8th December the Japanese hit Hong Kong and began their invasion of Malaya and Singapore. Attacking Hong Kong with 12 battalions of infantry and with overwhelming air cover, they rapidly pushed the British, Indian and Canadian troops out of the Kowloon peninsula. By the night of 18th December they were on Hong Kong Island itself. The entire British force surrendered on 26th December.③

① Liddell Hart, B. 'History of the Second World War', Pan Books, London, 1973, p. 209.

② Wasserstein, B. 'Secret War in Shanghai: Treachery, Subversion and Collaboration in the Second World War', Profile Books, London, 1998, pp. 7 – 8.

③ Endacott, G.B. 'A History of Hong Kong' 2nd ed. Oxford in Asia Paperbacks, Hong Kong, 1988, pp. 300 – 303.

第一节 日本偷袭

1941 年 12 月 7 日上午 7 时 55 分，日本空军袭击珍珠港美国舰队。等到第二波日本飞机飞回航空母舰时，已有大概 2500 名美国人死去，4 艘美国战舰被击沉，另外 4 艘被严重损坏。但对日本来说不幸的是，日军在发动空袭时，美国的航母恰好出海巡航，而正是这些航母在 6 个月后于中途岛重创日本帝国海军，使其一败涂地。

在日本偷袭珍珠港的 1 个小时后，他们开始袭击上海。在当地时间凌晨 4 时，日军登上了黄浦江上两艘仅存的非日军战舰，美国海军“威克”号和英国皇家海军“海燕”号在几分钟内向日本投降。

12 月 8 日，日本袭击香港并开始入侵马来西亚和新加坡。日军以 12 个步兵联队的兵力和势不可挡的空中掩护迅速将英国、印度和加拿大的军队逼出了九龙半岛。到 12 月 8 日晚，香港岛已完全被日军占领。英国军队在 12 月 26 日全体投降。

In Malaysia the retreat before the Japanese was almost continuous. By the beginning of January the British and their Australian allies had been pushed back to the Slim River near Kuala Lumpur. Japanese tanks soon broke through. The Indian 11th Division fighting with the British was shattered. The 30th January saw the British forces crossing into Singapore Island. By February 15th it was all over and 25,000 British and allied troops went into captivity. Few would survive the next three and a half years.[①]

For the Chinese inhabitants of Shanghai, Hong Kong and Singapore the long nightmare of the Japanese occupation had begun. Soon the Japanese were rounding up Chinese men in Singapore and executing them. In Hong Kong many of the population would be forced out of the territory by the Japanese and made to fend for themselves as best they could. In Shanghai, where so many of the Chinese population were refugees from the Japanese, there was now no escape.

6.2 Shipping losses soar

For the Chinese mariners in Liverpool the next few months were probably the worst period of the War. Such news as got through to them from the Far East was bad and getting worse and despite the entry of America into the conflict the losses at sea were growing.

---

① Lee Kwan Yew 'The Singapore Story: Memoirs of Lee Kwan Yew', Prentice Hall, Singapore, 1998, pp.44 – 48.

在马来西亚，盟军军队在日本军队面前一再退却。到次年1月初，英国及其澳大利亚盟军已被逼至吉隆坡附近的士林河。日军的坦克很快突破了防线，同英军一起作战的印度第11步兵师也被粉碎了。1月30日，英军被迫撤到新加坡。到2月15日，2.5万多名英军和盟军战士都被俘虏。在接下来的三年半时间里，他们历经折磨，只有少数人得以幸存。

对于上海、香港和新加坡的中国人来说，被日本占领的漫长噩梦开始了。很快日军将在新加坡的华人聚集到一起并处决了他们。在香港，许多中国人被日本人赶出香港领土，自谋生路。在上海，日军的烧杀抢掠造成了众多难民，现在他们无处可逃了。

第二节　船只损失激增

对于利物浦的华人海员来说，接下来的几个月可能是战争中最难熬的阶段。从远东传来的消息越来越糟，尽管美国已经加入战争，但海上的损失仍在继续增加。

Long range bombers needed to protect the merchant fleet from U-boats were being diverted to the bombing campaign over Germany. The frigates that were to be built in the USA to sail with the convoys were simply not being built. The Americans had given priority to landing craft they hoped to use in the invasion of Europe in 1943. Worst of all, the Americans were making life easy for the U-boats waiting off their coast.①

Reluctant to sail in convoys, the Americans placed no restrictions on the use of radio within their waters and continued to light their channel markers. These actions could not have been more helpful to the U-boat commanders looking for merchantmen. Best of all, when the U-boats located them the Americans ensured that they were clearly silhouetted against the miles of neon lights blazing away in their costal cities – and losses soared.

In February 1942 almost 500,000 tons of shipping was sunk. In March the figure exceeded 500,000 tons. In April there was a small decrease to 430,000 tons but in May the losses jumped to 600,000 tons. June saw the frightening figure of 700,000 tons of shipping go to the bottom of the sea. At this rate Britain was going to lose the war.②

The stress on all mariners was immense. And the Chinese were at breaking point.

---

① Liddell Hart, B. 'History of the Second World War', Pan Books, London, 1973, p. 39, p. 399.

② Ibidem, pp.400 – 401.

本来计划用来保护商船队免受U型潜艇危害的远程轰炸机被调去执行轰炸德国的行动。为了保护商船队，计划在美国建造的护卫舰迟迟没有开工，因为美国优先建造的是登陆舰，他们希望在1943年进攻欧洲时能将其投入使用。更糟糕的是，美国对游荡在其海岸线附近的U型潜艇放任自流。

美国海军不愿与护航船队一起航行，没有对美国水域中无线电的使用加以严格管理，也没有对导航助航设施进行管制，这些行为给正在搜寻商船的德国U型潜艇指挥官提供了很大的帮助。甚至当德国U型潜艇锁定到商船目标时，这些商船在沿海城市延绵数里的霓虹灯的映照下会清晰地显现出其轮廓，所以损失猛增。

1942年2月，被击沉的英国船只总吨位接近50万吨。3月，这一数字超过了50万吨。4月，略下降到43万吨，但在5月时又激增至60万吨。到6月时，沉入海底的船只总吨位已达令人恐惧的70万吨。按照这个速度，这场战争英国输定了。

所有的海员都承受着巨大的压力，尤其是中国海员，他们已经到了崩溃的边缘。

6.3 Trouble

Butterfield and Swire, like Holt, had strong links with Liverpool and, again like Holt, depended for much of their business on China. The vessels of their China Navigation Company plied their trade up and down the China coast from Hong Kong to Shanghai and beyond. With the fall of these ports to the Japanese, ships that had been successful in evading the Japanese began to arrive in Australia and India.

One of their steamers managed to get out of Hong Kong only to be bombed when the Japanese attacked the Philippines. With men killed and wounded, it reached Australia where its crew sent telegrams to the Australian Prime Minister John Curtin, the Chinese Ambassador Tsu Mo and the Chinese Consul General Tuen Mao-Lan asking for help. The company offered the men £5. Upset and insulted, they immediately contacted the Australian Seamen's Union requesting assistance.[①] The trouble that was to continue into the months ahead wherever there were Chinese seamen had begun.

By 22nd January 1941 a Chinese Seamen's Union, linked to the Kuomintang, had been formed in Sydney.[②] Before the month ended the crews of three of the China coast vessels in Sydney, the

① Translation of letter from Li Cheng, seaman, to Leung Kwan, wireless operator, 'SS Anhui' dated 15/1/1942; File C320/P1 Chinese Seamen's Union, Australian National Archives, Sydney, Australia.

② Letter from P.W. Ellestan, Controller of Postal an Telegraph Censorship to C/O Department of the Navy 'Chinese Seamen's Union Sydney'; File C320/P1 Chinese Seamen's Union, Australian National Archives, Sydney, Australia.

第三节　问题

与霍尔特公司一样，巴特菲尔德 & 施怀雅公司与利物浦也有着紧密的联系，而且它们的生意大多依赖于中国。它们在中国的船队原本在中国香港、上海沿岸及其周边地区往返贸易。随着这些港口被日本占领，这些船舶成功地避开日本人而到达澳大利亚和印度。

在日本进攻菲律宾时，巴特菲尔德 & 施怀雅公司的一艘轮船在设法驶出香港时遭到轰炸，造成船员伤亡。当这艘轮船到达澳大利亚时，船员向澳大利亚总理约翰·卡廷以及中国驻澳总领事段茂澜发电报请求帮助。公司后来只给了他们每个人5英镑。他们倍感失望和屈辱，随即联系了澳大利亚海员工会寻求帮助。

1941年1月22日,属于国民党的中国海员工会在悉尼成立。月底，停靠在悉尼港的三艘用于中国近海航行的船舶，“太平”号、“内洛尔”号和“安徽”号举行了罢工。澳大利亚军事情报局的报告认定这些罢工是早有准备的。

Tai Ping, Nellore and Anhui were on strike. Australian Military Intelligence was writing that it was certain that the strikes were being coordinated.①

Almost immediately the situation became violent. In Western Australia in the port of Fremantle the crew of the China coast ship the Chungking refused to work. Australian troops were sent on board. Shots were fired and two Chinese were killed.②

For those with relatives in China they were now unable to return home or to send money to their families. For those with family in the UK, wartime inflation was making life ever more difficult for their wives and children. The men were frustrated and angry. What is more, they were beginning to show it.

In Liverpool men whose two-year contracts had expired were refusing to sign on again. Offered £5 a month War Bonus and even two months pay as a signing on bonus they still would not re-join their ships.

In February 1942 the British Ministry of War Transport accepted that something had to be done. Negotiations had to be started between the shipowners, the Chinese Ambassador, Dr Wellington Koo, and themselves.

① Letter from Captain W. G. Reay, AHQ Liaison Officer, OSRA, Sydney to Director of Military Intelligence, Army HQ, St Kilda road, Melbourne, February 4th, 1942; File C320/P1 Chinese Seamen's Union, Australian National Archives, Sydney, Australia.

② Cable form Investigate, Perth to Fedcensor, Canberra, January 29th, 1942; File SP109/3 'Shooting of Chinese Seamen', Australian National Archives, Sydney, Australia.

情况随即演变为暴力冲突。在西澳大利亚的弗里曼特尔港口，一艘中国沿海船只“重庆”号上的海员拒绝工作，澳大利亚竟派遣军队登船并开火，两名中国人被杀。

对于在中国有亲属的人，他们现在不能回家也不能给家里寄钱。对于那些在英国有了家庭的人，战时通货膨胀使得他们妻儿的生活更加困难。这些人既沮丧又愤怒。渐渐地，他们的情绪开始表露出来。

在利物浦签订了两年劳工合同的中国海员合同已经到期，但他们拒绝续签。尽管每个月提供给他们 5 英镑的战争津贴甚至如果续签还另加两个月工资作为补贴，他们还是不愿再次上船工作。

1942 年 2 月，英国战时运输部决定采取措施。于是在船东、中国大使顾维钧博士以及战时运输部之间展开了一场谈判。

6.4 The negotiations

Educated at a Catholic school in Shanghai and with PhD from Columbia University in the USA, Wellington Koo was probably one of the few people who could bridge the cultural gap between the western powers and the Chinese.[①] It was now his responsibility to negotiate terms that would satisfy the Chinese seamen and not antagonise the British.

Dr Koo accepted early in the talks that the Chinese were not to have equality of pay with the British. The shipowners and the Ministry of War Transport agreed that the Chinese would get paid the War Bonus as long as British seamen were receiving it. Ironically, the Chinese were to eventually get effective pay equality with their British counterparts. But the War Bonus agreement did not survive the end of hostilities for the Chinese. As we will see, the British continued to receive it beyond the surrender of the Axis powers.

As the negotiations continued it emerged that Chinese seamen worked a 70-hour week – ten hours a day. Holt paid no overtime. Anglo-Saxon paid 4 pence an hour to lower ranked ratings and 6 pence an hour to the higher ranked. The equivalent of 1.5 pence and 2.5 pence in modern coinage. By mid March Anglo-Saxon were willing to increase overtime pay by 50% and increase the basic wage by thirty shillings a month-£1.50 today.[②]

① Craft, S.G. 'V.K. Wellington Koo and the Emergence of Modern China', University Press of Kentucky, Lexington 2004, pp. 8 – 21.

② File MT9/3743 Chinese Consul General, 'Chinese Seamen's Home', National Archives, Kew, UK.

第四节　谈判

曾经在上海天主教学校学习并在美国哥伦比亚大学取得博士学位的顾维钧，也许是为数不多能够连接西方列强与中国人之间的文化隔阂的人了。如何协调出一个既能让中国海员满意又不让英国人反感的条件，这个重担现在就落在他身上了。

顾维钧在早期谈话中显然认同中国海员没有得到与英国海员平等的工资。船东和战时运输部最后同意只要英国海员能拿到战时津贴，也就少不了中国海员的。中国海员终于能和英国同行得到平等的服务薪金，真是讽刺。但是战时津贴协议并没有消除中国海员的敌意。后来我们会发现，轴心国投降后英国海员仍然享受战时津贴。

谈判中显示中国海员一周工作 70 个小时，即每天 10 小时，霍尔特公司却没有付加班费。盎格鲁 – 撒克逊公司付给等级较低的海员每小时 4 便士加班费，等级较高的海员每小时 6 便士加班费。相当于现代货币的 1.5 便士和 2.5 便士。到 3 月中旬，盎格鲁 – 撒克逊公司愿意将加班费增加 50%，并且基本工资每个月涨 30 先令，相当于现在的 1.5 英镑。

The end of March saw Holt and Anglo-Saxon offering a £2 per month pay increase but still there was no agreement. Pay had been stopped for the striking mariners in mid-February and tension was increasing.

At the beginning of April the Chinese Consul in Liverpool Daniel Y Dao was advising the men not to join ships on the terms being offered. He was said to be telling them to demand that they be paid from 16th February, the date when pay had been stopped. That this had been agreed by the British on 5th March.①

Now came news of more violence towards the Chinese in Australia. Dutch marines had shot striking Chinese mariners in the port of Fremantle West Australia.② Tension between the Chinese, the shipowners and the British Ministry of War Transport reached a new high.

There was further violence by the Dutch towards the Chinese in Curacao where Chinese mariners sailing for one of the Dutch arms of Shell, the Curacao Scheepvaart Maatschappij, also struck. Again, the focus was pay. In particular the War Bonus. In March 1942 eight men seen as the ringleaders were arrested and imprisoned. The remainder of the Chinese demanded that they too be detained. Unable to force the men back to work, the Dutch authorities decided on a demonstration of force aiming machine guns at the recalcitrant Chinese. Reports differ as to what

① Ibidem.

② Cable form Investigate, Perth to Fedcensor, Canberra, January 29th, 1942; File SP109/3 'Shooting of Chinese Seamen', Australian National Archives, Sydney, Australia.

3 月末，霍尔特公司和盎格鲁 - 撒克逊公司每个月涨了 2 英镑工资，但双方仍然没有达成一致。并在 2 月中旬停发了罢工海员的工资，局势变得紧张起来。

4 月初，驻利物浦中国领事陶寅建议中国海员在这种待遇情况下不要再上船工作。据说他告诉他们要求公司从停发工资那一天，即从 2 月 16 日开始给他们开工资。3 月 5 日，英国人同意了这一要求。

更多关于在澳大利亚中国海员遭遇暴力的新闻传来。荷兰海员在西澳大利亚的弗里曼特尔港口射杀了罢工的中国海员。从而使中国人、船东以及英国战时运输部之间的紧张局势达到了一个新高峰。

荷兰海员对中国海员的暴力事件进一步升级。库拉索航运公司——壳牌公司的荷兰子公司，位于库拉索岛，在这个公司工作的中国船员也罢工了。焦点还是工资，尤其是战时津贴。1942 年 3 月，8 名被视为罢工带头者的中国船员被捕入狱，剩下的中国海员为了声援他们也要求被捕。在强迫他们回船工作不成的情况下，荷兰当局决定通过武力胁迫的方式，用机关枪瞄准拒不服从命令的中国海员。接下来发生的事情各方说法有所不同，但荷兰当局开火射杀，造成 12 名中国人死亡、44 人受伤。

happened next but the Dutch opened fire killing 12 Chinese and wounding 44 others.[①]

On 10th April 100 ratings had to be expelled by the police from the Anglo-Saxon offices in Liverpool.[②] Company staff attempting to recruit crews were said to have been threatened and one man, Ah You, had been beaten up when he attempted to sign on. It was being reported that contract expired men were doing all they could to stop ships leaving the Mersey.

On 11th April the Evening Standard newspaper reported that 200 Chinese seamen in Liverpool's Chinatown had thrown bricks at police and assaulted them. The police had tried to break up a protest meeting the Chinese were holding in the city's Cleveland Square opposite the Chinese Club.[③] The Chinese had collected bricks from a nearby bombed building and hurled them at the constables. Violence was becoming the norm.

And the violence was not restricted to Liverpool. With dozens of ships being sunk off the American eastern seaboard and with apparently no end to the discussions on their pay in sight, trouble with Chinese mariners was being reported in the USA. The Americans were convinced that the root cause was money–or rather the huge discrepancy in pay between the Chinese and British seamen.

① Drs. Junnes Sint Jago 'De Tragedie Van 20 April 1942', Imprinta Atiempo, Prins Bernhard Fonds N.A. & Aruba, Curacao, 2000.

② Lo, K.H.C. 'Forgotten Wave', Padiham Advertiser Ltd., Padiham, 1947, p.19.

③ Cutting from 'Evening Standard' newspaper in File MT9/3743 General 'Chinese Seamen's Home', National Archives, Kew, UK.

4 月 10 日，警察从盎格鲁－撒克逊公司利物浦分部驱散了 100 名普通船员。据传，公司试图招聘船员却受到威胁，一个名叫阿友的人在试图签约时被殴打。据报道称，这些合同到期的员工正尽一切所能阻止船只离开默尔西河。

4 月 11 日，《旗帜晚报》报道称 200 名在利物浦的中国海员朝警察扔砖头并且袭警。警察试图驱散一场中国人组织的抗议聚会，聚会地点在华人俱乐部对面的克利夫兰广场。中国人从附近的一个被炸的大楼捡了一些砖头并朝着警察扔去。暴力冲突已经成为了常态。

利物浦对这些暴力冲突束手无策。许多船只不断在美国东海岸被击沉，而关于中国海员工资的争吵也显然得不到什么结果，中国海员的问题在美国被报道出来。美国人认为问题的根源是钱的问题——或者说是中国海员和英国海员工资上巨大的差别。

The situation was now such that even the Chinese Seamen's Union in Liverpool was becoming concerned. Early in April 1942 T. S. Chen of the Union wrote to Foo Hee Chong of the MV Cymbula, an Anglo-Saxon vessel, about what was happening. He expressed sympathy with the men being, as he put it, 'exploited' by the shipping companies but called for an end to the strike.① Nor was the Union alone in its concerns. By 20th of the month Ambassador Soong in Washington was writing to Dr. Koo that '...it is in everyone's interest that the matter be speedily settled.'② An agreement had to be reached before things got completely out of hand.

With pressure coming from all sides the London Agreement was signed on 24th April 1942. The ordinary seamen were to get £2 a month increase in their basic pay and a re-signing bonus of two months pay at the new rate if they signed a one-year contract. Overtime pay was to be set at one shilling per hour, 5 pence for lower ratings and one shilling and three old pence for higher ratings. The War Risk bonus was set a £5 a month.③

But the men still would not go back to work. Such was the ill feeling that had been generated over the years that even after the agreement had been signed 500 seamen in Liverpool were still

① Telegram 9.4.42 translation of letter from T.S. Chun, Seaman's union, Liverpool to Foo Hee Chong 29.3.42; File MT9/3743 General 'Chinese Seamen's Home', National Archives, Kew, UK.

② Telegram from Ambassador Soong, Washington, USA to Dr. Wellington Koo, London, April 20 1942; Box 50 'Chinese Seamen 1942-47', Wellington Koo Collection, Rare Books and Manuscripts Library, Columbia University, New York, USA.

③ File MT9/3743 General 'Chinese Seamen's Home', National Archives, Kew, UK.

甚至利物浦中国海员工会现在也牵涉其中。1942年4月初，工会的陈泰星写信给在盎格鲁－撒克逊公司“贡多拉”号上工作的钟福喜讲述了发生的事情。正如他所说，他对这些海员被航运公司如此“剥削”的遭遇深表同情，但是也呼吁结束罢工。而且并不仅仅只有工会牵涉其中，4月20日，中华民国外交部长宋子文在华盛顿写给顾维钧的信中说道：“所有人都认为事态应该迅速解决。”于是在事态未完全失控之前，达成了一个协议。

在各方的压力下，《中英关于英籍航海船舶雇佣中国海员待遇及条件之协定》于1942年4月24日签订。普通海员每月基本工资涨2英镑，如果期满重新签订一年合同将按照新的工资标准发放两个月工资作为奖金。加班费每小时1先令，低级海员每小时5便士，高级海员每小时1先令3便士，战时津贴每月5英镑。

但是人们仍然不愿回去工作。由于多年来产生的反感，在协议签订之后利物浦还有500名中国海员拒绝上船工作。他们根本不相信已达成的协定。在加尔各答，中国海员也拒绝上船，所以不得已用印度海员替换了2000名华人海员。

refusing to join their ships. They simply did not believe that an agreement had been reached. In Calcutta men were also refusing to sail and 2000 Chinese seamen had to be replaced by Indians.

To make matters worse, no sooner had the London Agreement been signed than the War Risk money for British seamen was increased to £10 a month. Captain Glasier of Holt and M. W Rowbottom of Anglo-Saxon immediately contacted the Ministry of War Transport. The money for the Chinese must be increased to the same amount. The Dutch had already conceded it. Lord Leathers, the Minister for War Transport, refused. The British even writing to the Dutch to persuade them not to pay the additional War Risk money.①

Britain was now utterly dependent on the supplies coming across the Atlantic. If the ships did not sail, the U-boats' work would be done for them. Worried and exasperated, the British Merchant Shipping Mission in Washington weighed in to the argument in a telegram dated May 1st 1942 and sent to the Ministry. The Mission applied what pressure it could to Leathers writing that the Chinese negotiators would '...lose face badly when (they) see that one week after they obtain a rise of £2 for their seamen...your seamen get an increase of £5.'②

J.R Hobhouse of Holt wrote to Sir Julian Foley, the senior civil servant at the Ministry, on the same date as the Mission in the USA showing real insight into what was at the root of the Chinese

① Ibidem.

② Ibidem.

更糟糕的是，《中英关于英籍航海船舶雇佣中国海员待遇及条件之协定》签订后不久，英国海员的战时津贴就涨到了每个月 10 英镑。霍尔特公司的格莱希尔船长和盎格鲁－撒克逊公司的 M.W. 罗博顿船长随即联系战时运输部，说明中国海员的战时津贴也要涨到相同的数目。当荷兰人已经在考虑这个问题时，战时运输部大臣莱瑟斯勋爵却拒绝了这一请求，他们甚至给荷兰人写信，劝说他们不要支付额外的战时津贴。

英国现在全然依靠来自大西洋的补给。如果船只不航行，U 型潜艇将完成他们的工作。位于华盛顿的英国商船运输委员会既担心又恼火，1942 年 5 月 1 日，他们在一封发往英国战时运输部的电报中阐述了他们的观点。委员会在电报中尽可能地向莱瑟斯施加压力，写道中国的谈判代表会特别没面子，因为“在中国海员工资涨了 2 英镑的一周后，英国海员却涨了 5 英镑”。

霍尔特公司的 J.R. 霍布豪斯写信给运输部的高级文官——朱利安・福利爵士。而写信的当天正是位于美国的委员会真正地了解了中国海员不满的根源——平等。“比起别的事情，中国人更加重视平等这个观念，显而易见，从一开始战时津贴的

seamen's discontent – equality. '…the Chinese have attached more importance to the equality idea than to anything else, it has been obvious from the start that equality of War Risk money meant more to them than the mere cash…'①

Equality of War Risk money was conceded on 6th of May and soon men were signing on in 'good numbers...' in Liverpool. It had been conceded that they were men taking the same risks as British men, enduring the same conditions and suffering the same losses. For the moment, they were being treated as equals – almost. But the damage to relations between the Chinese, the British Government and the shipowners was now severe and permanent. The 'left wing agitators' had been noted and they and their families would pay a high price for their militancy when the War ended.

① Ibidem.

意义对于他们来说就不仅仅只是现金这么简单”。

5月6日，通过平等发放战时津贴，很快在利物浦就有很多中国海员签约。他们终于被承认是和英国人一样了，冒着同样的危险、忍受同样的处境并遭受同样的损失。在那一刻，他们得到了平等——几乎平等的对待。但是现在中国人、英国政府和船东之间的关系却遭受了严重而永久的破坏。那些“左翼煽动者”已经被盯上了，而且当战争结束时他们的家庭会为他们的斗争付出惨重的代价。

07

Chapter 7. A dangerous time

第七章　危险时期

The Chinese mariners had now got much of what they wanted. Equality of War Risk pay valued their lives as the lives of other men, but it was to be many months before the risks they faced were to lessen. It was not until the spring of 1943 that the Battle of the Atlantic turned in favour of the Allies. In the meantime the dreadful sinking of ships and killing of seamen continued.

By the middle of 1942 the Americans had finally accepted that convoys reduced their losses and on 19th July Admiral Donitz of the German Kriegsmarine ordered the last U-boats to withdraw from the United States Atlantic coast. However, increased U-boat production meant that he now had a total strength of 300 submarines of which half could be at sea at any one time. Of these, an increasing number were the so-called U-cruisers of 1,600 tons capable of sailing 30,000 miles before having to return to base. They were soon to prove themselves to be extremely effective killing machines.[①]

By the end of July Donitz had re-positioned his wolf packs off Greenland, the Canadian coast, the Azores, North-West Africa, the Caribbean and Brazil. But his main focus was the air escort gap south of Greenland – where the limited range of the Allied aircraft then available prevented them from covering the vulnerable merchantmen.

Escort vessels were being withdrawn to cover other aspects of the Allied war effort. The American troopship convoys taking

① Liddell Hart, B. 'History of the Second World War', Pan Books, London, 1973, p. 401.

中国海员已经得到了他们想要的大部分东西了。中国海员与其他国家的海员一样平等地享有战时津贴，这种津贴是对海员们生命价值的衡量。然而他们将经历长达数月的危险时期后才能逐渐脱离险境。直到 1943 年春天，大西洋海战出现了转折点，盟军取得了战争的有利地位。在这期间，沉船事故频发，无数海员丧命，令人心痛。

直到 1942 年年中，美国最终承认了护航队的存在减少了损失这一事实。同年 7 月 19 日，德国海军总司令邓尼茨下令，最后一批 U 型潜艇从美国大西洋海岸撤离。然而，U 型潜艇的增产意味着邓尼茨总司令已经拥有共计 300 艘潜艇，任何时间都会有一半的潜艇在海里服役。另外，新型的 1600 吨位的 U 型潜艇在数量上不断增加，它们的续航能力可以达到三万海里。不久之后，这些 U 型潜艇就被证明是极其高效的杀人机器。

同年 7 月底，邓尼茨上将重新部署了他在格陵兰岛、加拿大海岸、亚速尔群岛、非洲西北部、加勒比海以及巴西附近的“狼群战术”。但他的主要目标集中在空中护卫薄弱的格陵兰岛南部，盟军飞机在这里的覆盖范围有限，不能很好地掩护那些容易受到袭击的商船。

护卫船队的舰艇被调出来去掩护盟军在其他方面的作战力量。美国的战舰护卫队向英国输送步兵，并且从商船护卫队中抽调了数量庞大的护卫队。面对当时的情形，邓尼茨上将的战

the 'doughboys' to Britain took significant numbers of escorts away from the merchant convoys. Faced with this reality, Donitz's strategy meant that losses for the merchant fleet climbed immediately. Over half a million tons of shipping were sent to the bottom of the ocean in August. The sinkings continued at worrying levels for the rest of the year and by its end the Axis had sunk 7,790,000 tons of Allied shipping.[①] British imports had been reduced to only two-thirds of what they had been in 1939. People could tighten their belts – and did. But merchant ships needed oil and by December 1942 there was little more than two month's fuel for those vessels left. The tankers manned by the Chinese were becoming more important than ever and the Germans knew it.

The stormy weather of December 1942 and January 1943 gave some respite to the seamen on the merchant vessel as losses fell to around 200,000 tons. They doubled in February-and then came March 1943.

So many U-boats were now on patrol in the North Atlantic that it had become difficult for the convoys to avoid detection. In March the Germans altered their U-boat communication code and it was 10 days before the Allies could read it again. Convoys UGS6, HX228, SC121, SC122 and HX229 were badly hit. One hundred and twenty ships were sunk that month and hundreds of merchant seamen died. The casualty lists contain multiple entries with the words 'presumed drowned' opposite the names of man after man.[②]

① Ibidem p.403.

② RSSA/A/85-97 Register of Shipping and Seamen: Monthly List of Deaths of Seamen. Caid Library. National Maritime Museum, Greenwich, UK.

略意味着商船将遭受惨痛的损失。8 月，超过 50 万吨位的船舶沉入海底。在这一年余下的几个月中，沉入海中的船舶数量一直处于令人担忧的水平。到了 1942 年年底，在轴心国的攻击下，总计 779 万吨位的船舶沉入大海。此时英国的进口额只相当于 1939 年的三分之二。人们只能勒紧裤腰带，的确也只能这样。但是商船需要石油，到了 1942 年 12 月，可供这些船只使用的燃料最多只能撑两个月了。这样一来配备中国海员的油轮比以往任何时候都更重要，德国人也深知这一点。

1942 年 12 月和 1943 年 1 月，由于暴风雨天气，商船上的海员们得到喘息，本月船舶损失降低至 20 万吨左右。2 月损失翻倍，3 月损失依旧持续。

数量如此庞大的 U 型潜艇在北大西洋展开巡逻行动，因此商船队很难不被敌军发现。1943 年 3 月，德军改变了其 U 型潜艇的通讯编码，盟军直到 10 天之后才破译。UGS6、HX228、SC121、SC122 以及 HX229 船队都遭到了 U 型潜艇猛烈的袭击。120 艘船只沉入海底，数百名海员失去了生命。伤亡名单上很多人的名字旁都写着“可能溺亡”。

So bad were the losses in this month that the British Naval Staff began to wonder whether convoys really were an effective mode of defence for the merchant fleet.① The convoys were effective and, although the authorities did not know it, this was the turning point in the Battle of the Atlantic. Fifteen ships had been sunk in the last eleven days of the month. A sad and fearsome loss. But 107 ships had been destroyed in the first part of that awful month. In April the number of ships sunk halved. In May it was lower again. And May also saw 34 U-boats destroyed – 25% of their operational strength at the time. That month the slow convoy ONS 5, made up of 43 merchantmen and protected by 16 warships, was attacked by a pack of 30 U-boats. Six of the German submarines were lost. Two weeks later, convoy SC130 was attacked and a further 5 U-boats were sunk. The Americans were providing VLR (very long range) Liberator bombers to escort the convoys – and the Germans were losing the battle. Donitz wrote to Hitler that the losses were unsustainable. He withdrew his U-boats from the North Atlantic.②

The U-boats were never again to be the same threat to merchant seamen. Ships continued to be sunk but in much, much smaller numbers. By the end of 1943 the threat to the merchant fleet was over. The constant fear of the unseen underwater killer was gone.

For the Chinese mariners the fear of losing their lives may

① Liddell Hart, B 'History of the Second World War', Pan Books, London. 1973, p. 405.

② Fischer, K 'Nazi Germany: A New History', Constable and Company, London, 1995, p. 541.

这个月盟军损失非常惨重，以至于英国海军人员开始思考护航队到底能不能真正有效地保护好商船。实际上护航队是有效的，尽管当局当时并没有意识到这一点，护航队的有效防御也是大西洋海战的转折点。在 1943 年 3 月的最后 11 天里，15 艘船只沉海，损失令人感到悲伤和恐惧。但在这个月的前期有 107 艘船只遭到摧毁。4 月，沉船数量减少了一半。5 月，沉船数量再次降低，同时有 34 艘 U 型潜艇遭到摧毁，这是德军当时可用战斗力的四分之一。这个月，43 艘商船组成的 ONS 5 船队缓慢航行，由 16 艘战舰保驾护航，遭到 30 艘 U 型潜艇的袭击。德军损失 6 艘潜艇。两个星期以后，SC130 船队遭受袭击，又有 5 艘 U 型潜艇沉海。美国提供 VLR（超远程）解放者轰炸机来保卫船队，导致德国在这次战役中失败。邓尼茨上将写信给希特勒，表示损失惨重无法承受，他被迫将他的 U 型潜艇从北大西洋撤离。

U 型潜艇对于商船海员的威胁减小了，虽然还有船只在不断地沉入大海，但在数量上比之前少了很多。到了 1943 年年底，U 型潜艇不再对商船构成威胁。人们对于一直以来看不见的水中杀手的恐惧感也消失了。

中国海员不再担心他们的人身安危了，但三条战线的战争在中国还在继续。日本占领下的中国腹地很少传出消息，但从

have diminished to vanishing point but the three-way war in China continued. Little news was coming out of the territories occupied by the Japanese but the news coming out of the areas still held by the Nationalists or Kuomintang was, as ever, bad and getting worse.

7.1 Back home

The Americans had heavily damaged the Japanese Imperial Navy at the Battle of Midway in June 1942 and begun their island-by-island march to Japan with their bloody conquest of Guadalcanal. But this brought little respite to the people of China.

The Japanese now attacked into Zhejiang, the Province next to Shanghai. The Nationalists were bringing Chinese to the battle roped together to stop them running away. Medical facilities were scant or non-existent and, as was all too often the case, casualties were immense.[①]

Natural disasters added to the misery with floods, locust plagues and crop failures sweeping the country. In Henan no rain fell anywhere in the Province in 1942 but the Nationalists took up to 50% of what little food was available. Two million died in the resulting famine with the dead carpeting the roads and the living resorting to cannibalism to stay alive.

In the town where the Party had been founded, Shanghai, the

① Fenby, J. 'Modern China: the Fall and Rise of a Great Power, 1850 to the Present', HarperCollins, New York, 2008, p. 306.

国民政府或国民党统治下的区域传出的消息，照旧是坏消息，而且情况变得越来越糟糕。

第一节　回家

1942年6月，美军在中途岛战役中沉重打击了日本帝国海军，并在瓜达尔卡纳尔岛血战后，随即开展“跳岛行动”，但这并没有给战争中的中国人民带来喘息的机会。

不久，日本攻占了邻近上海的浙江省。国民党将中国壮丁押送到前线，用绳子将他们绑起来以防止其逃跑。由于多数情况下医疗设备短缺甚至无法供给，伤亡人数非常庞大。

自然灾害更加剧了人们的痛苦，洪水、蝗灾以及农作物歉收席卷了中国。1942年，整个河南省内滴雨未下，但国民政府却征收了河南省仅有的少量食物中的一半。这导致200万人死于饥荒，饿殍遍野，为了生存，甚至出现了人吃人的情况。

1942年夏天，中国共产党的成立地上海，由于日本管理体系的崩溃，爆发了一场严重的霍乱。当时整个中国，物价

summer of 1942 saw the outbreak of a severe cholera epidemic as civil governance broke down under the Japanese. As seemed to be happening throughout China, inflation roared ahead and food shortages grew worse and worse.① The Chinese population entered a dark world that would engulf them for many decades into the future.

Hardship and brutality was the lot of those still living in Hong Kong and it continued throughout the occupation. Many were forced out of the Territory to seek what help they could in the villages over the border. But the resistance of the Cantonese population to the Japanese invader continued. They carried messages into the prison camps from the British and Hong Kong resistance group over the border in Guangdong Province. Made up of British military personnel plus Chinese and Eurasians from the Hong Kong Volunteer Defence Corps, the so-called British Army Aid Group in Free China relied for their effectiveness on the resistance movement in Hong Kong. The local Cantonese passed food to civilian prisoners from what little they had and risked their lives in helping military prisoners to escape.② In Sai Kung in the New Territories they conducted their own guerrilla war against the Japanese occupiers. Fighters killed Japanese soldiers and buried the bodies standing up. This so that those walking over them would insult them in death by standing on their heads.

---

① Wasserstein, B. 'Secret War in Shanghai: Treachery, Subversion and Collaboration in the Second World War', Profile Books, London, 1998, p. 110.

② Ride, E 'British Army Aid Group: Hong Kong Resistance 1942-1945', Oxford University Press, Hong Kong, 1981, pp. 31 – 32.

飞涨，食物短缺，情况越来越糟。中国人陷入了一个黑暗的世界里，并将影响他们数十年。

依然生活在香港的人们也尝尽艰辛，苦难和残暴弥漫在日本占领区。很多人被迫离开香港，越过边境，在邻近的乡村谋生。但广东人依然在不断抵抗日本侵略者。他们跨越广东省的边境，将英国和香港抗日团体的消息传递到战俘集中营内。英国军队人员、香港义勇军中的中国人和欧亚混血儿组成了英军服务团，服务团在中国这片自由的土地上能够存留下来是因为在香港的抗日活动中发挥了作用。当地的广东人把他们仅有的少量食物送给平民俘虏，还冒着生命危险帮助他们逃脱。在香港新界的西贡区，他们与日本侵略者开展游击战。战士们杀死日本士兵，将他们的尸体竖着掩埋，这样经过的人们就会踩着他们的头羞辱他们。

In Singapore and Malaya Force 136, trained by British officers, operated from the jungles on the peninsula but few Malays joined the fight. It was Chinese guerrillas, some Communist, some Nationalist who fought against the Japanese throughout the War. Inspired by Chinese nationalism,① the Communists were to prove as big a problem to the British after the War as they had to the Japanese during it. That was in the future. A future that in 1942 and 1943 looked bleak indeed.

7.2 Fairness, equality and human dignity

The signing of the London Agreement did not mean the end of disputes between the British Ministry of War Transport, the shipowners and the Chinese mariners on Merseyside. Nor did it lead to harmony in Australia or other parts of the World. The dispute had fundamentally damaged the relationship between the Chinese and their employers. Chinese cultural values meant that the Chinese mariners believed that their loyalty to their employer should have been met with reciprocal loyalty to them. For them the relationship was not and could not be one that was purely monetary. J.R Hobhouse of Alfred Holt had shown real understanding when he had told Sir Julian Foley that the issue of War Risk money was not about finances but about equality of treatment. Giving the men 'face', affording them the dignity of being treated as fellow humans.

① Lee Kwan Yew 'The Singapore Story: Memoirs of Lee Kwan Yew', Prentice Hall, Singapore, 1998, pp.86 – 87.

在新加坡和马来亚的136部队[1]，由英国军官负责训练，他们在半岛的热带雨林中与日本人展开战斗，但只有少量马来人加入。这是典型的中国式游击战，一些共产党人和国民党人在整个战争中一直坚持与日军战斗。共产党人深受民族主义鼓舞，他们对于战争之中的日本人，以及战争之后的英国人都是一个大问题。未来情况就是这样。实际上，根据1942年和1943年的情况来看，共产党的前景是非常黯淡和渺茫的。

第二节　公正、平等以及人权

《中英关于英籍航海船舶雇佣中国海员待遇及条件之协定》的签署并不意味着英国战时运输部、船东以及默西赛德郡的中国海员之间的争执得以消除，也没有调和澳大利亚以及世界上的其他地区之间的矛盾。中国海员与船东之间存在的争端严重影响了彼此之间的关系。中华文化价值观促使中国海员认为自己对船东的忠心也应该相应地换来船东对自己的坦诚相待。对于中国海员来说，他们和船东之间的关系不是也不可能仅仅是金钱上的联系。霍尔特公司的J.R.霍布豪斯对这一点认识得很透彻，他向朱利安·佛利长官说道："战时津贴不仅仅是经济问题，也是平等待遇的问题。"给中国海员脸面，让他们像其他人一样得到保全他们自尊心的待遇。明白了这一点，船东所关注的海员福利就不仅仅是物质上的，还包括人权方面的问题。

---

① "二战"期间英国军方组建的一支代号为136的特种部队，主要任务是渗透到马来亚本土做颠覆和破坏工作，为收复马来亚、新加坡做准备，中国方面先后选送了一百多人参加136部队，英方负责训练、装备、运送和指挥联络。——译者注

Showing that, as employers, they cared for the welfare of the men not just in material but human terms.

Lord Levers had, of course, shown the very opposite of this in his initial refusal to grant the Chinese the same increase in War Risk money as the British when their payment was raised from £5 to £10 per month.① Levers did this with a perfection of timing that was positively awe inspiring – if he wished to demonstrate a lack of concern for Chinese sensitivities.

The extent to which personal dignity was at the core of the matter was shown when Chinese members of an Anglo-Saxon tanker refused to serve with men who, in their view, were being over-paid. From a telegram from the Chinese Consul in Bombay to Dr. Wellington Koo in June 1942, we learn that crew members who had served many years with the company would rather leave the vessel they were on than serve with the newcomers. It was not 'fair' and they would not stand for it.②

Fairness and equality of treatment continued to be a problem in Australia even after the London Agreement. Chinese crews of British vessels based in Australia found that the Agreement still left them working under conditions far worse than the Australians facing the Japanese enemy. Paid significantly less than the

---

① Telegram from the Foreign Office to Chungking, January 21st, 1942. Repeated to Washington; File MT9/3743, National Archives, Kew, UK.

② Telegram from Chinese Consulate, Bombay to Chinese Embassy, London, June 21st, 1942; Box 50 'Chinese Seamen 1942-47', Wellington Koo Collection, Rare Books and Manuscripts Library, Columbia University, New York, USA.

很显然，莱威尔勋爵表现得与之截然相反。当英国海员的战时津贴由每月 5 英镑涨到 10 英镑时，他最初拒绝为中国海员提高同等涨幅的战时津贴。如果莱威尔想要显示他并不在意中国海员的感受的话，那么他这样做确实是选对了时机，因为他的行为确实刺激了中国海员敏感的神经。

一艘壳牌石油公司油轮上的中国海员拒绝与在他们看来薪资过高的船员一同工作,这是他们为了个人的尊严在进行抗议。1942 年 6 月，在孟买的中国领事给顾维钧博士发来一封电报，从这封电报中，我们了解到那些在船上工作数年的海员宁肯放弃船上的工作，也不愿意与新来的船员[①]一同工作。他们无法容忍这种不公平待遇。

即使在《中英关于英籍航海船舶雇佣中国海员待遇及条件之协定》签署之后，公正和平等待遇的问题在澳大利亚依然存在着。在澳大利亚往来的英国船上的中国海员发现，《中英关于英籍航海船舶雇佣中国海员待遇及条件之协定》的签署依然令他们处于非常糟糕的工作环境中，这种环境比澳大利亚人面对日军时的境况还要糟糕很多。中国海员的薪水远远少于澳大利亚人。他们每星期需要工作 56 个小时，而澳大利亚人只需要工作 44 个小时。这不可避免地导致了问题的出现，中国海

① 指用来替换中国海员的印度海员。——译者注

Australians,① they were having to work a 56 hour week whilst the Aussies only put in 44.② Inevitably this caused problems as crews refused to work in protest. Understandably, the Chinese wanted to be treated as men equal to any others.③

The problems continued and Justice J. A. Ferguson was asked to conduct an inquiry into the employment of Chinese seamen in Australia. On 31st March 1943 he presented his report. It made the seemingly obvious point that as long as the Chinese were paid less than the Australians they would continue to feel '…they were being treated unfairly'. ④ Amazing as it may seem this was apparently still not obvious to the shipowners. Equality of treatment would make no difference they said. In a letter to Thomas Gordon of the British Ministry of War Transport in Sydney, one Captain J. V. Van Nooraken wrote that the only way to deal with the Chinese was to jail them.⑤ Indeed, some had already been imprisoned but with no obvious affect. They continued to insist that they should be treated as others were treated.

Alfred Holt eventually bowed to the inevitable in May 1943.

---

① Memo from High Commissioners Office, Australian Government, London, August 4th, 1942; File 472/6 Australian National Archives, Canberra, Australia.

② Letter from Shell Company Australia, Melbourne to Ministry of War Transport, Sydney, March 27th, 1943; File 472/6 Australian National Archives, Canberra, Australia.

③ Note to file; FileCO4177 Australian National Archives, Canberra, Australia.

④ Report by J.A. Ferguson, March 31st, 1943; File W9495 'National Security (Inquiries)', Australian National Archives, Canberra, Australia.

⑤ Letter from Captain J.V. Van Noorden, Liaison Officer, Water Transport Division to Thomas Gordon Representative in Australia for the Ministry of War Transport, Sydney January 29th, 1943; FileA472/6 Australian National Archives, Canberra, Australia.

员通过罢工来抗议。这也可以理解，中国人想要得到和其他国家的人一样的平等待遇。

问题一直在持续。J.A. 弗格森法官受命对在澳大利亚工作的中国海员开展了一场调查。1943 年 3 月 31 日，弗格森公开了他的调查报告。报告明显地指出：只要中国海员的薪资低于澳大利亚人，他们就一直会觉得受到了不公正的待遇。但令人感到惊讶的是，面对如此明显的事实，船东却置若罔闻。他们认为中国海员是否能得到平等的待遇意义不大。英国战时运输部的托马斯·戈登曾在悉尼收到 J.V. 万·诺瑞肯船长写给他的一封信，信中说对付中国人唯一的办法就是将他们关到监狱里。实际上，已有中国海员被投入监狱，但这并没有取得明显效果。中国海员依然坚持他们应该得到与其他国家的人同样的待遇。

1943 年 5 月，阿尔弗雷德·霍尔特终于作出让步。从这一天起，该公司在澳大利亚的中国海员得到了每个月 8 英镑的薪资，这要比《中英关于英籍航海船舶雇佣中国海员待遇及条件之协定》上规定的还要高，并且他们还平等地享有同澳大利亚商船海员一样的战时津贴。然而不幸的是，对于利物浦华人社区，阿尔弗雷德·霍尔特公司已经公开名单，打算处理那些他们眼中“闹事儿的人”。尤其是对于上海人，正如我们后来看到的那样，战后那些上海人因坚持争取自己的人权而

From that date it began paying its Chinese crews in Australia £8 a month more than the London Agreement and gave them equality of War Risk money with Australian merchant seamen. Ominously for the Anglo-Chinese community in Liverpool the company had already put in print that they intended to act against those they saw as 'troublemakers'. In particular, the Shanghai men and, as we shall see, after the War the Shanghainese were to pay a high price for their insistence on being afforded some human dignity.

7.3 Equality at last?

It was not only in Australia that mid-1943 saw the Chinese finally achieve pay equality with their local counterparts. As of 1st February 1943 the pay of a British ordinary seaman was increased by £1.7.6 (£1.38). Once again, this seemed to demonstrate an absolute indifference to Chinese sensibilities. In reality it was probably due more to ignorance than deliberate intent. However, when Dr. Koo raised the matter with Lord Leathers in June of that year Leathers '...simply would not hear of the word equality...'① It was only when Dr. Koo reminded him that the principle had already been accepted that he agreed to take action. Once again Wellington Koo had to fight the good fight on behalf of his fellow Chinese who by now were convinced they would never get fair treatment.

① Telegram from Dr. Wellington Koo to T.V. Soong, Ambassador, Washington, June 7th, 1943; Box 50 'Chinese Seamen 1942-47', Wellington Koo Collection, Rare Books and Manuscripts Library, Columbia University, New York, USA.

付出了惨痛的代价。

第三节　中国海员最终获得了平等吗?

1943 年年中，在澳大利亚工作的中国海员终于得到了与当地海员同样的薪资待遇。1943 年 2 月 1 日，英国普通海员的薪资又上涨了 1 英镑 7 先令 6 便士（即 1.38 英镑）。同样的情况再一次发生了,这似乎显示出对中国人诉求的彻底漠视。而实际上，更多的是无意的忽视，而不是蓄意所为。然而，当顾维钧博士于同年 6 月向莱瑟斯勋爵提出这个问题的时候，莱瑟斯勋爵表示“不想听平等的字眼”，当顾维钧博士提醒他，他之前早就接受了平等这一原则后，莱瑟斯勋爵才表示会采取行动。顾维钧不得不为他的那些其实永远也不会受到公正待遇的中国同胞展开一次又一次的谈判。在美国，中国海员受到高工资的诱惑，背弃了原来的英国雇主，被招募到生产战争物资的美国公司工作。

In the USA they were being recruited to work in American war production factories and, lured by the high wages available, they were deserting their British employers to do just that.①

By September of that year Koo had managed to get the British to agree to an increase of £1.2.0 (£1.10) a month. An increase that brought the monthly pay of a Chinese mariner to £11.10.0 (£11.50) plus a series of special benefits not available to the British seamen. Koo argued that, given that the Chinese would pay no tax and the British would do so, they had finally achieved equality.②

For hundreds of Chinese this was welcome news indeed. Many of the younger men, assuming that they would not be going back to China for many years, if ever, now had local women as their partners. Increasingly these unions were producing children. That last great flowering of the Anglo-Chinese community that was to produce a thousand children. Tragically, most of them were never to know their fathers.

① Letter from O. Becu, New York to J.H. Oldenbrook, London, April 27th, 1943; File 159/3/9/9, International Transport Workers Federation, Modern Records Centre, University of Warwick.

② Telegram from Chinese Embassy London to Sino mission, Washington September 16th, 1943; Box 50 'Chinese Seamen 1942-47', Wellington Koo Collection, Rare Books and Manuscripts Library, Columbia University, New York, USA.

到了 1943 年 9 月，顾维钧成功地说服英国人同意为中国人每月增加 1 英镑 2 先令（即 1.10 英镑）的薪水。工资上涨后，中国海员每个月可以拿到 11 英镑 10 先令（即 11.50 英镑），并且享受英国海员所没有的一系列特别福利待遇。对此，顾维钧说：鉴于中国海员不需要交税，而英国海员需要交税，所以中国海员最终和英国海员享受到了平等的待遇。①

对于成百上千名中国海员来说，这真是一个好消息。很多中国青年海员设想在很长时期内他们不会回到中国，如果可能的话，他们会娶当地的女子作为人生的伴侣。越来越多的这种结合孕育出了很多孩子。这是华人社区最后一次人口高峰，大约 1000 名孩子诞生。但悲剧的是，大多数孩子都没有时间也没有机会去认识和了解自己的父亲。

① 这里是指英国海员的工资仍旧比中国海员高一点，但英国海员需要交所得税，而中国海员没有相关税，所以实际上中英海员之间的工资待遇差不多。—— 译者注

08

Chapter 8. The beginning of the end

第八章　战争结束前期

By the beginning of 1944 the war against Germany and Japan was moving towards its end. In the Far East the Americans were pressing the Japanese military back ever closer to their homeland. The Germans were on the retreat before the Red Army and within six months the great D-Day landings would take place in France. British and American bombers were reducing German cities to heaps of smoking rubble. But the cost to all involved, German and Allied alike, was heavy.

On 14th January 1944 a Lancaster bomber crashed into woods 5 kilometres south of Stockse in Germany. Sergeant Ronald Soo of Liverpool died along with four other members of the crew. Born in the city in 1920, his father, Ah Kwong Soo, was a seaman. His mother was Beatrice Whittam. His brother, Frank, had played football for England.① Liverpool's Anglo-Chinese community was very much part of Britain and it was making the same sacrifices as every other part of the nation. But what of the city itself?

At sea fewer ships were being sunk and supplies and men were getting through to Britain from America as the preparations for D-Day continued. The docks where the men and materials landed had been damaged and repaired but the damage to the city itself had not been repaired. It would not be for many years to come. The city was in poor shape. It was a city that few who now live there would recognise.

The Liverpool of that time was a place of terraced houses

① 'Chinese Community – Liverpool and Merseyside Remembered' http://www.bbc.co.uk/ww2peopleswar/stories/79/a3904779.shtml.

到了1944年年初，盟军同德国和日本的战争已逐渐接近尾声。在远东地区，美国将日军节节逼退至日本本土，德国人在苏联红军面前也节节败退，6个月后，“诺曼底登陆”彻底扭转了战局。英军和美军的轰炸机将德国的城市炸成硝烟中的一堆堆瓦砾。但包括德国与盟军，所有参战国付出的代价都是惨重的。

1944年1月14日，一架兰卡斯特轰炸机坠入德国斯道克斯以南5公里的树林中。来自利物浦的罗纳德·苏中士和其他四名机组人员一同阵亡。罗纳德·苏在1920年出生于利物浦，他的父亲苏光亚是一名中国海员，他的母亲名叫比阿特丽斯·威特姆，他的哥哥弗兰克曾经代表英格兰参加过足球比赛。利物浦华人社区是英国不可缺少的一部分，也像英国其他各个地区一样遭受着损失。但这座城市本身又怎么样了呢？

被击沉的船只越来越少，物资和人员也源源不断地从美国运往英国，这一切都在为诺曼底登陆作准备。人员和物资登陆地点的码头遭到破坏后被再次修复，但对这座城市其他地方的破坏却没有得到修复，甚至很多年后依旧没有改善。整座城市破败不堪，居住在此的也很少有人能认出这座城市。

那个时期的利物浦有很多成排的房屋，矗立在默西河畔的山脉上，从山脚向高处依次分布。屋内没有卫生间和浴室，除

climbing up the hill from the river Mersey. Houses that had no inside toilets or bathrooms, no heating other than a coal fire and certainly no hot water supply. Like most of the city's buildings, those houses had been blackened by the smoke and soot pouring out of chimneys all over the town. From the houses themselves and from the factories that were producing the materials to fight the war.

Those houses fronted directly onto cobbled streets where children played undisturbed by traffic. The fathers of many of those children were, of course, in the military or, more likely in the port of Liverpool, in the Royal Navy or merchant marine. Increasingly the sharp eyed observer could notice that some of these children had the dark hair, almond shaped eyes and golden skin of Liverpool's Anglo-Chinese.

Liverpool was ending the War with a severe housing problem. The city had had some of the worst slums in Europe before the War started and the attempts by the German Luftwaffe to knock out the port had made the situation worse. Much, much worse. Anyone looking down and across the river could see the damage. The city centre had been all but erased from the map. Whole streets had been bombed flat. Thousands of houses damaged. Families lived in one room or shared with relatives. The Liverpool authorities knew that the problem would grow rapidly worse as its men returned home when the War ended. They would have to take action. Sadly, some of the actions they would take would affect the lives of the Anglo-Chinese through to the present day.

了煤火没有其他取暖设备，当然也没有热水供应。与城市里的大多数建筑一样，这些成排的房屋都被城镇里烟囱冒出来的烟雾和烟灰熏黑了，居住屋和工厂里都在为战争生产军用物资。

这些房屋前面是由鹅卵石铺就的街道，孩子们在这里玩耍，没有来往车流的打扰。很多孩子的父亲是在部队工作，或者也可能在利物浦港口、皇家海军或是商船上工作。渐渐地，细心的人可以注意到这些孩子中有一些与利物浦的英籍华人一样，长着黑色的头发和杏仁儿眼，有着黄皮肤。

随着战争的结束，利物浦出现了严峻的住房问题。在战争开始以前，这座城市就分布着一些欧洲最破败的贫民区，德国空军空袭这座港口后，情况变得愈发糟糕。当俯视全城或是经过默西河，都能目睹战争给这座城市带来的破坏。市中心差一点就从地图上消失了。轰炸机将所有的街道夷为平地，无数房屋遭到破坏。一家人同住在一间屋子里，或者与亲戚挤在一起。利物浦政府明白问题很快就会变得更加糟糕，因为战争一结束人们就会重返家园。所以政府不得不采取措施，但悲哀的是，政府所要采取的一些措施将会影响到英籍华人的生活，而且这种影响将一直持续到今天。

But it was not just the happenings in Britain that were determining the fate of the community. Just as important for its future and that of its children was what was happening in China. For what was happening in China would impact on the fate of the fathers of the community's children. In particular, the men who came from Guangdong and Shanghai. The offensive the Japanese were about to start would not only reduce parts of Guangdong to starvation but it would severely weaken the Nationalists in their struggle against the Chinese Communist Party.

8.1 Ichigo

In spring 1944 the Japanese launched Ichigo, their biggest single offensive of the War in China. Ironically, it was aimed not at the Chinese, although they were to suffer immensely from it. It was targeted at the American air bases in Eastern China. Bases from which the USAF was launching the bombing raids that were destroying Japan city by city.[①]

The Japanese Imperial Army swept across the Yellow River in Henan Province to the northwest of Shanghai. As they retreated before the Japanese onslaught, Chinese Nationalist forces were attacked by the local peasants. Desperate for revenge for the treatment they had received from the Nationalists, they turned on their tormentors burying alive Chinese troops as they tried to flee

① Fenby, J. 'Modern China: the Fall and Rise of a Great Power, 1850 to the Present', Harper Collins, New York, 2008, p. 300.

华人社区的命运不仅受到英国国内事件的影响，也受到中国国内事件的影响。因为发生在中国的事情将会影响到华人社区孩子们父亲的命运，尤其是影响那些来自广东和上海的人的命运。日本人即将开展的进攻不仅会让广东地区的老百姓挨饿，而且也会严重削弱与共产党斗争的国民政府的实力。

第一节　一号作战

1944 年春天，日本人发起一号作战计划，这是他们在中国发动的最大规模的战役。但令人感到讽刺的是，一号作战并不是针对中国人的，虽然中国人在这场战争中遭受了巨大的伤害。它的目标实际上是位于中国东部的美国空军基地，因为美国空军基地对日本实施轰炸袭击，摧毁了日本的一座座城市。

日本帝国陆军的铁蹄在河南省跨过黄河到达上海西北部。由于国民党在日军进攻前就撤退，国民政府的军队遭受到当地农民的袭击。这些农民迫切想要报复国民党以前对他们的所作所为，于是他们展开了袭击行动，活埋那些企图在日本进攻前逃跑的国民党军队。

before the Japanese.

By the end of June the Japanese had taken the American base in Hunan Province, hundreds of miles from their jump-off point. Subsisting on no more than two bowls of rice a day and with no heavy weapons, the Nationalist Chinese Tenth Army held the Japanese for seven weeks. At the end of the battle only 300 men survived to fight their way out.

The Japanese had reached Kweilin, 200 miles further south and almost at the southern extremities of China by autumn. Torching the city, they turned north towards Chungking in Sichuan Province, the wartime capital of Nationalist China. They halted at last in the mountains at Dushan.①

The offensive had reduced southern China to a state of utter wretchedness. Towns had been burnt to the ground and such roads as existed were crowded with refugees. Guangdong Province, of which Hong Kong is historically a part, and from which many Liverpool's Chinese seamen originated, suffered its worst cholera outbreak since 1932.

Ichigo had cost the Nationalists hundreds of thousands of men. The offensive had over-run all the factories that Chiang Kai-shek had ordered removed from the east in the 1930s. His government was weaker than ever. Even so, he was already preparing for a full-scale resumption of the conflict with the Communists.

Chiang now signed a Sino-Soviet agreement with Stalin that

① Fenby, J. 'Generalissimo Chiang Kai-shek and the China He Lost', The Free Press, London, 2003, p. 431.

到了6月底，日军已经占领了位于湖南省的美军基地，该基地距离日军的进攻地点有数百英里。中国国民党第十军的士兵们在一天不足两碗米饭、没有重型武器的情况下硬撑着，将日军拖了七个星期。在战役结束时只有300名士兵活下来，并突围出去。[①]

日军南下200公里抵达桂林，到了秋天，他们几乎占领了中国的最南端。他们放火烧城，转而北行，向国民党的战时首都，即地处四川省的重庆进攻。最终日军在独山山脉停止前行。

日军的进攻使中国南方遭受严重摧残。战火将城镇烧为平地，道路上挤满了难民。在历史上，香港曾是广东省的一部分，很多利物浦的中国海员也来自广东省，现在广东遭受了自1932年以来最为严重的霍乱。

"一号作战"消灭了几十万的国民党军队。日军的此次进攻迫使国民党所有的工厂超负荷运转，这些工厂是蒋介石在20世纪30年代下令从东部搬迁过来的。此时蒋介石政府变得前所未有的脆弱，但即便如此，蒋介石也已经准备与共产党重新展开全面斗争。

现在蒋介石与斯大林签署了《中苏友好同盟条约》，这份

① 即长衡会战。其中，方先觉率领第十军坚持47昼夜之衡阳保卫战，是抗战史上极为惨烈的一场孤城保卫战。—— 译者注

gave the Soviets joint use of the Manchurian railways and the use of Port Arthur as a naval base. In return, the Soviets recognised Manchuria as part of China and the Nationalists as the government of China.[①] This done, Chiang began to move huge numbers of troops north to reinforce those already facing the Communists.

In Shanghai itself raids by American heavy bombers from mid-1944 onwards so damaged the power stations that electricity was available only a few hours a day. These raids and Japanese rapaciousness had, by early 1945 reduced the city's manufacturing output to barely a quarter of its 1937 level. The transportation system had all but disintegrated and food shortages were now acute. Money had become worthless.[②] A situation that was to occur yet again under the Nationalists when the War ended.

Many of Hong Kong's pre-war population were now in China or dead. The busy city of 1,650,000 people had been reduced to no more than 600,000. A million souls had fled from the territory or had been driven out of Hong Kong by the Japanese. They had crossed the border into China but many had died on the way. Hundreds had been dumped by the Japanese on islands with no water supply. Hong Kong's famous Happy Valley racecourse had been turned into a vegetable garden as the desperate population tried to survive. Corpses were rotting in the streets.[③]

---

① Ibidem pp.450-451.

② Wasserstein, B. 'Secret War in Shanghai: Treachery, Subversion and Collaboration in the Second World War', Profile Books, London, 1998, p. 256.

③ Lindsay, O 'The Battle for Hong Kong 1941-1945: Hostage to Fortune', Spellmount, Stroud, 2007, p. 223.

协定赋予苏联人对满洲铁路的联合使用权，并允许苏联人将阿瑟港（旅顺港在西方的称呼）作为海军基地。作为回报，苏联承认满洲是中国的一部分,并承认国民政府是中国的合法政府。条约签完后，蒋介石开始向北方调遣大量军队，增援那些已经与共产党展开对抗的军队。

从1944年年中开始，上海遭受到美国重型轰炸机的袭击，发电厂受到严重损坏，一天只有几个小时可以供电。空袭加上日军的掠夺，1945年年初上海市的制造业产量仅仅是1937年的四分之一。交通运输系统近乎崩溃，而且食物严重短缺，货币贬值。战争结束后，在国民党掌控下，这种情况将会再次出现。

很多香港人在战争爆发后来到中国大陆，有的已经离世。在香港这座繁忙的城市中，原来高达165万的人口缩减到不足60万。100万人从香港这片土地上逃离或是被日本人驱逐出境。他们穿越边境来到中国大陆，有很多人在途中就去世了。日本人将很多香港人丢弃在小岛上，不给他们供水。腐烂的尸体在街道上随处可见。为了生存，香港著名跑马地的赛马场变成了菜园子。

The situation was scarcely better in Singapore. Clothes were being made out of curtains. People were eating old, musty rice supplemented by anything remotely edible. The majority of the men who worked for Anglo-Saxon Petroleum had been recruited from Singapore. Numbers of these men were members of the Communist Liverpool Chinese Seamen's Union and they too were taking Liverpool partners and having children. At the end of the War their political beliefs and those of the Shanghai men would cost them and their families dear as the Communists became the new enemy.

8.2 The shipping companies get ready

Until the outbreak of World War Two ,the British shipowners carrying cargo around the world had operated a cartel. They did not call it a cartel, of course. Rather, they gave it the innocent-sounding title of the 'British Liner Committee'. The Committee agreed the rates they would charge their customers and parcelled out the world and its commercial traffic between its members. Given the size of Britain's Empire at the time and the dominating position of her merchant fleet, their position had seemed unassailable. That is, until the War. That had completely altered things for the shipowners – and they knew it.

From the early years of the conflict the members of the Committee had been expressing increasing concern about their

新加坡的情况也没有多好。人们穿着用窗帘制成的衣服，吃着陈年发霉的大米，并在米里掺杂任何可以吃得下肚的东西。在壳牌石油公司工作的大多数中国海员都是从新加坡招募的。他们中的很多人是共产党领导的利物浦中国海员工会的成员，他们也和利物浦的姑娘结婚生子。在战争结束之际，他们以及上海人的政治信仰将会让自己及家人付出惨痛的代价，因为共产党人成为了新的敌人。

第二节　轮船公司准备就绪

第二次世界大战爆发以前，在世界各地营运的英国船东成立了卡特尔，当然，那时不称其为卡特尔，而是取了一个听起来很不着边际的名字“英国班轮委员会”。委员会确定他们应该向托运人收取的运费并推广到全世界，同时在会员船东之间协调商业运力。鉴于当时大英帝国的国土面积以及其商船船队的垄断地位，英国船东的地位似乎无法撼动。直到“二战”爆发后，英国船东的垄断局面才得到彻底改变。

在战争初期，船东委员会的成员表示他们担心在战争结束时的竞争力。巨大的船舶损失让他们最高效的船舶也沉入海底。

ability to compete when peace finally came. The massive shipping losses were sending their most efficient vessels to the bottom of the ocean. To replace them the Americans were building huge numbers of so-called Liberty ships. They may have been ugly and utilitarian but they were efficient and they were numerous.

As we have seen, the year 1942 had been a dreadful one for the merchant marine with almost 8 million tons of shipping destroyed. But despite these horrendous losses the shipowners were planning their post-War operations and the picture they could see worried them. On 17th December 1942 an anxious Martin Hull of the Liner Committee wrote to J. R. Hobhouse of Alfred Holt. We have already come across J. R. Hobhouse in the wage negotiations with Dr. Wellington Koo earlier that year. Hull's concern was that there would be a '...surplus of tonnage over post-war requirements.' That is, too many ships chasing too little business.[1]

Hull wanted to strike a deal with the Americans to, as he put it, '...sterilize...' this likely surplus of vessels to '...bring the fleets of the Allies...into more normal proportionate relationships.'[2] In other words, incorporate the Yanks in the cartel so that the cosy 'I scratch your back, you scratch mine' pre-war situation could be maintained. Hobhouse, possibly with the costly negotiations with Dr. Koo still fresh in his mind, seemed to be growing pessimistic

---

① Letter from Martin Hull, British Liner Committee to J.R. Hobhouse, December 17th, 1942; Box QA311, J.R. Hobhouse World War Two Papers – Policy 1943-44, Ocean Archive (Holt), Liverpool Maritime Museum, Liverpool, UK.

② Ibidem.

为了取代他们，美国人建造了大量的自由轮。这类货轮也许外形丑陋，有些功利[①]，但非常高效，而且数量庞大。

正如我们所看到的，1942年对于商船来说是糟糕的一年，商船遭受到将近800万吨的损失。虽然损失骇人，但船东们正计划着他们的战后行动，而他们能够预见到的景象令他们感到担忧。1942年12月17日，英国班轮委员会的马丁·赫尔写信给阿尔弗雷德·霍尔特的员工J.R.霍布豪斯，表达了他对战后的焦虑。我们已经提到J.R.霍布豪斯在此之前曾与顾维钧博士进行薪资谈判。赫尔担心“战后运力过剩”，也就是说，船只过多，但生意却很少。

赫尔想与美国人进行一场交易，就像他所说，让这些战后可能剩余的船只“陷入一种无用的状态”“使盟军的船只达到合理的比例关系”。换句话说，让美国佬加入卡特尔中，这样，战前那种礼尚往来、互惠互利的美好局面将会持续下去。也许霍布豪斯依旧清晰地记得与顾维钧博士谈判所付出的惨重代价，所以他对未来比较悲观，他深信美国人将不会与之合作。

① 即当时自由轮做工粗糙，普遍认为一艘自由轮只要能完成一次美国到英国的航行即可。—— 译者注

about the future. He was firmly of the view that the Americans would not play ball.

As the end of the conflict drew near the shipowners worries increased. The neutral Swedes had a fleet of new and highly efficient vessels. Worse, they now knew that the Americans were definitely '...not willing formally to recognise any vested interest of established lines.'① There was now the possibility, if not the real likelihood of '...undesirable post-war friction if competition was allowed.'② The cartel was not used to competition nor geared up to face it.

With the end of the War approaching the shipowners faced a situation that was completely new to them. Alfred Holt, in particular, saw itself as under threat. Not only were they likely to face real competition, their cheap Chinese crews were no longer cheap. They determined to act and one more of the factors that were to affect the lives of many hundreds of Anglo-Chinese war babies in Liverpool swung into place.

① Draft letter to Ministry of War Transport 2.1.45; File OA 311British Liner Committee, Ocean Archive (Holt), Liverpool Maritime Museum, Liverpool, UK.

② Letter from Director of Stanley and John Thompson Ltd to Lord Leathers of MOWT September 20th, 1944; File OA311311British Liner Committee, Ocean Archive (Holt), Liverpool Maritime Museum, Liverpool, UK.

随着战争结束的临近，英国船东们的担忧却越来越强烈。中立的瑞典人拥有了一批崭新而又高效的船只。更糟的是，他们现在知道了美国人肯定“……不会认可任何航线上的既得利益者”。如果在允许竞争和人们不期望战后发生摩擦的情况下，那么会有这种可能性。卡特尔的建立本不是用于商业竞争，而且卡特尔也无法做好面对竞争的准备。

随着战争渐渐接近尾声，对英国船东们而言，他们面临着一种全新的情况，尤其是阿尔弗雷德·霍尔特公司，感受到了威胁。其不仅可能会面临真正意义上的竞争，而且他们廉价的中国海员现在也不再廉价。英国船东决定采取行动，而其采取的行动将使数百名在利物浦的“战时中英混血儿童”的生活受到严重影响。

09

Chapter 9. Of no further use

第九章　不再具有价值

By the end of World War Two, over thirty thousand merchant seamen had died, Twenty thousand Chinese sailing in Britain's merchant fleet had been based in Liverpool. We do not know exactly how many of them died. The names of some of the Chinese casualties are etched on the Merchant Navy memorial on Liverpool's waterfront. But if a quarter of all mariners were killed, a simple calculation shows that there were many Chinese deaths.

Hundreds of those who had survived now had partners and children on Merseyside. But the men were no longer needed to help fight the war and soon the issue of what to do with them and how to do it were being discussed at the highest levels.

By October 1945 with the war safely over notes in Government files begin to talk of 1200 surplus Chinese seamen① and of the need to remove them from the country. On 19th October 1945 officials from the Home Office and the Ministry of War Transport met with the Liverpool Chief Constable and immigration officers to discuss what could be done. The Chinese had now become '...an undesirable element in Liverpool...' ②

And the change had come so quickly. So very, very quickly. At the beginning of the year S.E. Dudley of the Home Office had been writing anxiously about the shortage of Chinese seamen for vessels going to the Far East war theatre. Of the fact that of all

① Note to file. Initialled F.A.N and C.E. Dated October 19th, 1945. File HO 213/926, National Archives, Kew, UK.

② Note of meeting held at Home Office: October 19th, 1945 – Repatriation of Chinese Seamen at Liverpool; File HO 213/926, National Archives, Kew, UK.

到第二次世界大战结束时，已经有 3 万多名商船海员失去生命。2 万名在英国商船上工作的中国海员主要集中在利物浦。我们不知道他们死亡的确切人数。一些离世的中国海员的名字被刻在了利物浦滨海区的武装商船纪念碑上。但如果说四分之一的海员失去生命的话，一个简单的估算就可以知道这其中有多少中国海员失去了生命。

很多幸存下来的中国海员随后在默西赛德郡结婚生子，他们不再需要帮忙打仗了，不久之后高层就会讨论如何处置他们及怎样实施。

到了 1945 年 10 月，随着战争顺利结束，政府文件的内容开始关注剩余的 1200 名中国海员，政府要将他们赶出英国。1945 年 10 月 19 日，内政部及战时运输部的官员与利物浦警察局局长及移民局官员见面，一同商榷采取何种措施以驱逐中国海员。中国人现在成为了“利物浦无价值的一分子”。

与战时相比，英国对待中国海员的态度发生了剧变。在年初时，内政部的 S.E. 达德利还焦虑地写道：能够登船前往远东战场的中国海员数量短缺。事实上，在利物浦的诸多海员中，似乎只有不超过 150 名海员是想逃避责任、被迫出海的，剩下的海员都已经或即将出海。

the thousands of seamen in Liverpool there seemed to be no more than 150 shirkers who could be pressed into service. The rest were already at sea or soon to be so.

April saw the Mercantile Marine Office in Liverpool telling the Ministry of War Transport that, if there shirkers, men who were a problem, it was certainly not the Liverpool Chinese mariners. It was the men that the Ministry had brought in from India and South Africa. It was those groups that contained the undesirables. ①

Around the same time the Ministry of War Transport in London was telegraphing its offices in Bombay praising the Chinese. Describing how Alfred Holt had been using '…complete Chinese crews...'② on the almost suicidally dangerous convoys to the island of Malta. How they had given loyal service supporting the fighting in North Africa, Sicily and Italy.

But now the war was over. The men could be safely got rid off and, as to their wives, it seemed they counted for nothing. After all, '…many were of the prostitute class and would not wish to accompany their husbands to China.'③ There was no need to consider them in the discussions.

And Liverpool City Council had higher priorities than the Chinese seaman, their wives and their families. Before the war

---

① Telegram to N.A. Guttery, MWT from W.A. Johnson, Mercantile Marine Office, Liverpool 1, Dated April 16th, 1945; File MT9/4125, National Archives Kew, UK.

② Telegram to MWTR, Bombay from SHIPMASTER, London, Dated March 6th, 1945; File MT9/4125, National Archives, Kew, UK.

③ Note of meeting held at Home Office: October 19th, 1945 – Repatriation of Chinese Seamen at Liverpool; File HO 213/926, National Archives, Kew, UK.

4月，利物浦商船局告知战时运输部：如果有想要逃避责任、制造麻烦的人，那么也一定不会是利物浦的中国海员，而是战时运输部从印度及南非引进的海员。这些人群才是不受欢迎的。

差不多在同一时间，伦敦的战时运输部也向其孟买的办事处发出电报，赞扬中国人。电报描述了阿尔弗雷德·霍尔特是如何雇佣“全部中国海员”配备在充满毁灭性危险的驶向马耳他岛的船队上。电报还描述了中国海员对公司的忠诚，支持英国在北非、西西里岛以及意大利的战斗。

但现在战争结束了，中国海员就可以被顺理成章地赶出英国了，至于他们的妻子，似乎无足轻重。毕竟，“她们当中的很多人是妓女，而且也不愿意陪着她们的丈夫远赴中国”。根本没有必要将她们的感受列入考虑范围内。

利物浦市议会不会考虑中国海员、海员的妻子和家人的感受。战争爆发前，利物浦市只有几百名中国人。现在这里却多了很多中国人，由于利物浦港口遭到了德国空军的严重损毁，“利物浦当局急于得到中国人所占房屋的使用权”。无论他们是拥有这些房产，还是只是和他们的家人居住于此，很显然都无关紧要。

there had been only a few hundred Chinese in the city. Now there were many, many more and, with the port having been heavily damaged by the German Luftwaffe 'The Liverpool authorities were anxious to secure the use of the housing accommodation which the Chinese occupied.'① Whether they owned these properties or lived there with their families was, apparently, an irrelevancy.

9.1 A difficult issue

How to get rid of these men?

The Home Office was certainly of the view that with the end of the war against Japan deportation orders could be issued to the Chinese mariners. But the police had to specify for each case, '... the grounds on which you think deportation would be justified...'② Certainly, a man could not be deported for failing to report for allocation to a ship or for a mere gambling offence or for smoking opium.③ The Police had repeatedly said that the Chinese involved no others in these activities and caused no trouble by them.

Home Office officials had records of no more than '...some dozen Chinese gangsters, brothel keepers and opium traffickers against whom there are specific grounds for deportation.' ④ The

① Ibidem.

② Letter from J.H. Sheet, Home Office, to The Commissioner of Police of the Metropolis, November 9th, 1945; File HO 213/926 National Archives, Kew.

③ Note of meeting held at Home Office: October 19th 1945 – Repatriation of Chinese Seamen at Liverpool; File HO 213/926, National Archives, Kew, UK.

④ Note of meeting held at Home Office: October 19th 1945 – Repatriation of Chinese Seamen at Liverpool; File HO 213/926, National Archives, Kew, UK.

第一节 一个难题

怎样来清除这些中国人?

内政部当然同意战争结束后将驱逐日本人的法令施加到中国海员身上。但警方需要具体说明每一件事例，即“驱逐所基于的正当理由”。当然，中国海员不可能因为没有到分派船只报到遭到驱逐,也不会仅仅因为赌博犯罪或者吸食鸦片而流放。警方一再声明，中国人在参与这些活动时没有影响到其他人，而且也没有为自己惹出什么麻烦。

至于放逐的具体理由，内政部的官员无外乎只是记录“一群中国人做黑帮、开妓院、做毒品贩子，为了杜绝这些活动而将他们驱逐”。利物浦警察局局长可以想出更多的理由。他认为有 18 名中国人的驱逐理由是合理的。那些参与犯罪活动或是严重违反船上纪律的中国海员应该被驱逐。那年 3 月，7 名海员因向英国境内走私鸦片而遭到逮捕和监禁。他们被判决服刑六个月到两年不等,这些中国海员毋庸置疑应该被赶出英国。另外 11 名海员也因自身的行为而从中国海员后备队的名单里剔除。船东一般从海员后备队中雇佣人手。包含中国大使馆代

Chief Constable of Liverpool could think of a few more. He was aware of 18 men whose deportation could be justified. Men who had been involved in criminal activity or in extreme indiscipline on board ship.① Seven seamen had been arrested and imprisoned in March of that year for smuggling opium into the UK. Given sentences of between two and six months they could undoubtedly be thrown out of the country.② So too could the eleven whose behaviour had caused them to be expelled from one of the Chinese Seamen's Pools. The labour pools from which men were recruited for sea duties. The Chinese Investigation Committee, which included representatives of the Chinese Embassy, had written to the Ministry of War Transport recommending their deportation at the end of April.③ But that hardly made a dent in the numbers. What do to about the rest?

The only solution the authorities could think of was to alter the men's landing conditions. In other words, the terms under which they were allowed to be on shore. The landing conditions could be changed so that they would be required to leave the country by a fixed date. If they failed to leave by that date, they would be clearly in breach of their landing conditions and could then be deported – simple!④ All that the authorities would have to

① Note to file. Initialled F.A.N and C.E. Dated October 25th, 1945. File HO 213/926, National Archives, Kew, UK.

② Letter from G.W, Guthrie, MWT to S.E. Dudley, Immigration Branch, Home Office, March 31st, 1945: File 213/808, National Archives, Kew, UK.

③ Letter to MWT c/o Alfred Holt and Co., from The Chinese Investigation Committee signed V. Hamilton, April 30th, 1945; File 213/808, National Archives, Kew, UK.

④ Note of meeting held at Home Office: October 19th 1945 – Repatriation of Chinese Seamen at Liverpool; File HO 213/926, National Archives, Kew, UK.

表的中国人调查委员会已经给战争运输部写信，提议在 4 月末将这些海员驱逐。但这 18 名中国海员微乎其微，留在英国的中国海员总数几乎没有减少。那么剩下的人该怎么办呢?

政府所能想出的唯一解决办法就是改变中国海员的登陆条件。换句话说，就是改变许可他们上岸的条例。登陆条件改变了，那么中国海员就需要在指定的日期离开英国。如果他们在规定的日期内没有离开，那么他们就明显违反了登陆条例，很简单，之后他们就会被驱逐。政府仅仅需要将这些持有海员证书的中国海员送到利物浦移民局。一旦他们到了移民局，他们就得更改护照，声明他们必须在某一特定的日期前乘坐指定的船只离开。

do was to have the men go to the Immigration Offices in Liverpool bringing their seamen's papers. Once they were there they would have their passbooks altered to say they had to leave on a specified day and on a specified ship.①

The authorities could now get on with organising the details of the repatriation. Lists of men could be drawn up. Departure dates set. Deportation orders could be drawn up for any men who failed to comply.② A theoretical sailing date would be set that was two days before the actual sailing date. Those who voluntarily went on board would not be allowed to leave the ships. Any who failed to report to the ships could then be rounded up by the police. Deportation orders would be prepared in advance for the police to use.③ Ships would shortly be available for the repatriations. The Ministry of War Transport could have some basic structural alterations made to the ships so that they could take men instead of cargo.④

9.2 The Great Round Up

By mid-November the repatriation was under way. Men were being called in to have their passbooks altered and soon

① Note to file. Initialled F.A.N and C.E. October 25th, 1945. File HO 213/926, National Archives, Kew, UK.

② Note to file. Initialled C.P.H. October 30th, 1945. File HO 213/926, National Archives, Kew, UK.

③ Note of meeting held at Home Office: October 19th 1945 – Repatriation of Chinese Seamen at Liverpool; File HO 213/926, National Archives, Kew, UK.

④ Ibidem.

有了大致原则，政府现在开始研究遣返中国海员的操作细节。首先，他们草拟了遣返人员名单，离开日期也已经定好，驱逐令可以为任何不遵守命令的中国海员起草。理论上的开航日期比实际上的开航日期要提前两天。那些自愿登船的海员不准许下船。任何没有登船报到的人之后都会遭到警方的拘捕。政府会提前为警方准备好驱逐令，遣返中国海员的船只也会在短时间内准备好。战时运输部会对船只的结构做出一些基本的改造，这样船只就可以载人而不是载货。

第二节　大逮捕

到了 11 月中旬，遣返中国海员的行动开始全面展开。海员们被召集起来，更改他们的护照，不久政府就安排一艘霍尔特的船只于 12 月 8 日将 100 名中国海员从利物浦运往新加坡。英国政府急于驱逐中国海员，搜刮他们的财物，然后将他们监禁起来。在中国大使馆进行强烈的抗议后，英国当局才停止了这种野蛮的、企图向中国海员施加压力的行径。

arrangements had been made to use one of Holt's vessels to ship out 100 men from Liverpool to Singapore on 8th December.① Anxious now to get rid of the men, the authorities had been collecting their possessions and locking them away. Only after vigorous protests from the Chinese Embassy did they cease this crude attempt to exert more pressure on the men.②

On 14th December, another Holt ship, 'Menelaus', sailed from Hull with 107 men. They had been collected from Liverpool and transported across the country. Eleven of the eighteen who could be deported went on this vessel.③

By now 300 men had been called in and processed and we start to hear of the plight of the men who had settled in Liverpool. They had been living with their partners for years. They had had children together. Desperate not to be forced apart, they had married as soon as the men had been told they would have to leave. Their cases were now '...being considered by the Police pending a report to the [Home Office].' ④

On 23rd March 1946 the Immigration Officer in Liverpool, Mr J. R. Garstang wrote to His Majesty's Chief Inspector that, up to that point, 800 men had been repatriated to Hong Kong, Singapore

① Letter to HM Chief Inspector from I. Holmes, Immigration Office, Liverpool, November 26th, 1945; File HO 213/926, National Archives, Kew, UK.

② Letter to H.M. Inspector, Liverpool from S.E. Dudley Immigration Branch, Home Office, London: November 23rd, 1945; File HO 213/926, National Archives, Kew UK.

③ Letter to H.M. Chief Inspector from J.R. Garstang, Immigration Office, Liverpool, December 15th, 1945: File HO 213/926, National Archives, Kew, UK.

④ Ibidem.

12 月 14 日，另一艘霍尔特的船“梅内莱厄斯”号从赫尔起航，搭载着 107 名中国海员。这些海员是从利物浦集中起来的，然后横穿英国。在之前被驱逐的 18 名海员中，有 11 名乘坐过这艘船。

那时，已经有 300 名中国人被召集起来并接受审查，人们慢慢知道了定居在利物浦的中国海员所面临的困境。他们已经与伴侣在一起生活很多年了，而且他们还有孩子。由于极度不希望被迫分离，中国海员在刚被告知将会离开英国时就与他们的伴侣结婚。“警方现在正在考虑他们的情况，并准备向内政部提交报告”。

1946 年 3 月 23 日，利物浦的移民官 J.R. 加斯唐先生给国王陛下的总督察写信，信中说截止到当时的时间点，已经有 800 名中国海员被遣送到新加坡、香港以及上海。另外的 1993 名海员也已经签署了遣返到远东的协议。换句话说，他们已经开始了单向航程。越来越多的在英国结婚的中国海员被驱逐离境。

and to Shanghai. A further 1993 men had signed articles for discharge in the Far East.① In other words, they had undertaken a one-way trip. We shall hear more of this when we consider the fate of the married men.

The number of men now remaining in the UK had been dramatically reduced in a relatively short period of time. By March 1946, Anglo-Saxon Petroleum could report that only 400 men remained. Holt reported that just 1500 of those who had sailed on their vessels were still in the country. And plans were afoot to ship out even more.②

Between March and Garstang's next report on 15th of July, a further 562 men were repatriated and another 1576 signed on for those one-way trips. Anglo-Saxon had no more men in the UK. Holt would be in the same position by the end of August.③ It was all over. The men had gone. But what of those with families? What had happened to them?

9.3 What to do with the married men?

Initially, it was agreed that married men would not have deportation orders made against them.④ Not much of a concession.

① Letter to H.M Chief Inspector from J.R. Garstang, Immigration Office, Liverpool, March 23rd, 1946; File HO 213/926, National Archives, Kew, UK.

② Ibidem.

③ Letter to H.M. Chief Inspector from J.R. Garstang, Immigration Office, Liverpool, July 15th, 1946: File HO 213/926, National Archives, Kew, UK.

④ Note of meeting held at Home Office: October 19th 1945 – Repatriation of Chinese Seamen at Liverpool; File HO 213/926, National Archives, Kew, UK.

留在英国的中国人的数量在很短的一段时间内急剧减少。到了 1946 年 3 月，壳牌石油公司报告称只剩下 400 名中国人。霍尔特报告称那些曾在该公司轮船上工作的中国海员中只剩下 1500 人还留在英国，而英国还在计划着将更多的中国人遣返出去。

加斯唐先生于同年 7 月 15 日又做了另一份报告，从 3 月到那时，又有 562 名中国海员遭到遣返，另外 1576 人签订了单程航行的协议。壳牌石油公司不再有大量的中国人了。到了 8 月底，霍尔特船舶公司的情况也是如此。一切都结束了。中国人离开了。但有家庭的那些人怎么样呢？他们发生了什么？

第三节　结了婚的中国海员怎么办？

起初英国政府同意不向已婚的中国男人下达驱逐令。然而政府没有做出太多的让步，正如我们所看到的，合法驱逐令的实施对象实际不超过 18 人。

As we have seen, deportation orders could be made against no more than eighteen men anyway.

Then this agreement was watered down a little. Men with British born wives and families should not be included in the first list of those to be forcibly repatriated. They should be reported on individually.① The social class of the women would, of course, have to be taken in to account.② Presumably this meant that those deemed to be of a low social class would see their husbands deported. Those men with wives considered to be of sufficient social status would be allowed to remain.

Then came further criteria for judging whether couples should be separated. Length of residence in the UK was added to the list.③ And, of course, just because a man was married to a British woman did not mean that his landing conditions should not be altered. He should still have his passbook marked as requiring him to leave.④ Nor should men married to British women be given any indication that this would give him any right to remain in the UK.⑤

That married men had been and were being repatriated must not be admitted. To do so '...might embarrass the Immigration Officer, Liverpool, the Police and the shipping companies...'⑥ But

① Note to file. Initialled C.P.H. Dated October 30th, 1945. File HO 213/926, National Archives, Kew, UK.

② Note to file by S.E.Dudley. Dated May 31st, 1946; File HO 213/926 National Archives, Kew, UK.

③ Letter from J.H. Sheet, Home Office, to The Commissioner of Police of the Metropolis, November 9th, 1945; File HO 213/926, National Archives, Kew, UK.

④ Letter to H.M. Chief Inspector from J.R. Garstang, Immigration Office, Liverpool, November 14th, 1945: File HO 213/926, National Archives, Kew, UK.

⑤ Ibidem.

⑥ Note to file by S. E. Dudley. Dated August 27th, 1946; File HO 213/926, National Archives, Kew, UK.

之后这项提议在人们的心里就有些淡化了。拥有在英国出生的妻子及家人的中国海员不在第一批被强制遣返的行列中，他们被单独上报。当然，其妻子的社会地位也作为参考因素。这大概意味着那些被视为属于底层社会的女人就得眼看着她们的丈夫被驱逐。而妻子被认为有着较高社会地位的中国海员就允许留下来。

后来又出台了其他评判夫妻是否应该分开的标准。在英国居住时间的长短也加在了评判标准中。当然，虽然中国海员娶了英国女人,但并不意味着他们的登陆条件就不需要做出改变。他的护照上依然标记着需要离开。与英国女人结婚的中国海员并没有得到任何有权留在英国的暗示。

那些已经被遣返和正在被遣返的已婚中国海员一定是不允许留下来的。如果留下来的话，可能会令移民官、利物浦、警察以及航运公司陷入尴尬的境地。但有些已婚的中国海员暂时留了下来，他们还没有被强制赶出英国。

some married men had hung on. They had not yet been forced out.

The shipping lines added to the pressure. The major shipping companies were now offering to the Chinese mariners rates of pay that were approximately half of what they had been during the War.① Holt, in particular, were anxious to keep their supply of cheap labour. They were leaning on other shipping companies not to offer better rates of pay to any British-based Chinese seamen.②

The Immigration Officer in Liverpool, J. R. Garstang wrote to London in protest at what was happening. The men with families in the city particularly concerned him. He wrote to his superior officer in London that '...if a man signs on such Articles he cannot hope to support his wife in this country...' The women would be '...forced to go to China with her family i.e. she is compelled to leave the United Kingdom...' ③ But if he did not sign, or if he did not accept repatriation to China, he would receive no pay at all.④ Metaphorically, a gun was being placed to his head.

If a man refused to go to sea, he was not to be allowed to take a job ashore. Chinese seamen were to be '...discouraged...' from doing so. If that did not work, they would simply not be allowed to land to take up a shore job.⑤ That doing this was an act of bluff

① Letter to H.M Chief Inspector from J.R. Garstang, Immigration Office, Liverpool, August 20th, 1946; File HO 213/926, National Archives, Kew, UK.

② Ibidem.

③ Ibidem.

④ Note to file by S. E. Dudley. Dated August 27th, 1946; File HO 213/926, National Archives, Kew, UK.

⑤ Ibidem.

除了政府部门，航运公司也在向中国海员施加压力。现在，主要的航运公司为中国海员所提供的薪资只接近其战争期间薪资的一半。尤其是霍尔特公司，因急于保持公司的廉价劳动力而对其他的航运公司施加压力，不让它们向在英国船上工作的中国海员提供更高的薪资。[①]

利物浦移民官 J.R. 加斯唐先生给伦敦写信抗议所发生的事情。尤其是在利物浦已经有了家庭的中国男人牵动着他的心。他在给伦敦上司的信中写道："如果一个海员签订了这样的条款，那么他在这个国家就无望养活他的妻子。"女人也会"和她的家人一起被迫前往中国，也就是说，她被迫离开英国"。但如果海员不签订条款，或者不接受遣返回中国，那么他将不会得到任何薪资。打个比喻，这就如同用枪对着他的头。

如果中国海员拒绝出海，那么他将不被允许在岸上工作。这样一来，中国海员就"灰心丧气"，乖乖上船。如果这一举措不起作用的话，那索性就不许中国海员登陆，也就不能从事陆上工作。坦率地说，这种做法是一种处在非法边缘的行为。内政部官员明白，如果中国人坚持强调他们的要求，那么他们就能够上岸并将可以得到留在英国的签证。当然，这种情况发生的可能性几乎为零。

---

① 霍尔特公司此时采取的是将战争期间的中国海员遣返，而雇佣新的海员的策略。因为战争期间中国海员的工资高，而雇佣新的海员，公司可以把工资降低。——译者注

verging on the illegal was freely admitted. Home Office officials knew that if a man pressed his claim he would have to be allowed ashore and could readily obtain a visa to remain. The likelihood of this happening was, of course, remote.

Hundreds of British women now found themselves without their husbands and partners. Children lost their fathers. But how many suffered in this way? And who were they?

成百上千的英国女人发现她们没有了丈夫或伴侣，孩子失去了他们的父亲。但到底有多少人在遭受着这种失去亲人的痛苦？他们又是谁？

10

Chapter 10. Torn apart

第十章　分离

We will probably never know how many women and children now found themselves without partners and without fathers. Certainly, the British Government did not know. Was it 57 wives who had been separated from their husbands as S. E. Dudley of the Home Office wrote in August 1946? Or was it 74 as he had believed in June?① Perhaps the real number was 117? The figure that had been bandied around when forcing the men out of Britain had first been discussed.② Had 22 women really gone back to China with their husbands? Dudley thought so – but nobody seems to have known or to have checked. Like the men, these women seem to have disappeared into thin air. There is no further mention of them in the British records or in the Municipal Archives of Shanghai, the city to which they may have gone.

Was the number 150? Was it more? The national daily paper, the News Chronicle, reported that there were at least 150 women involved in a protest meeting in Liverpool in August 1946.Their husbands had been compulsorily repatriated and they had been left destitute. Yet the local Liverpool newspaper 'The Echo' reported that the meeting had double that number.③ That is, 300 women.

Whatever the number, it was obvious that many hundreds had been affected. And many, many children too. The newspapers

① Note to file by S. E. Dudley. Dated August 27th, 1946; File HO 213/926, National Archives, Kew.

② Note of meeting held at Home Office: October 19th, 1945 – Repatriation of Chinese Seamen at Liverpool; File HO 213/926, National Archives, Kew.

③ No author cited; 'British Wives of Chinese: A Wage and Living Crisis' in Liverpool Echo, August 19th, 1946.

我们也许永远不会知道到底有多少女人失去了丈夫，有多少孩子失去了父亲。英国政府当然也不知道。是否就像内政部的S.E. 达德利在1946年8月写的那样，有57名妻子与她们的丈夫分开？或者是达德利在6月时所认为的74名？也许真正的数字是117，这是人们第一次讨论政府将中国海员赶出英国时四处传播的数字。真的有22名女人和她们的丈夫一起回到中国了吗？达德利是这么认为的，但这个数字并没有被核实和调查过。与她们的男人一样，这些女人似乎也消失得无影无踪。英国政府的记录中再也没有提及她们，她们也许会前往的城市——上海市的档案馆里也没有关于她们的更多记录。

这个数字是150吗？是更多吗？英国一份全国发行的日报——《新闻纪事报》报道称，至少有150名女人参与了1946年8月在利物浦举行的抗议会议。她们的丈夫被强行遣返，使她们陷入贫困中。但利物浦当地报纸《回声报》却报道称有两倍的女人，也就是说，有300名女人参与了此次抗议会议。

不管数字是多少，很明显，有数百名女人受到影响。而且很多很多的孩子也受到了影响。报纸报道称每个女人平均有三个孩子。有些女人有六七个孩子。现在，很多年轻人实际上成了孤儿。为了生存，这些女人或孩子不得不跟随她们的丈夫或父亲去中国。女人和孩子也同样面临着“被强行派遣到我们并不想去的外国领土上”的境遇。即使女人和孩子知道男人的去

reported that the women had an average of three children each. Some had six or seven. Hundreds and hundreds of youngsters who were now, in effect, orphans. To live these families would have to follow their husbands and fathers to China. They too faced '... enforced deportation to a foreign land to which we do not want to go.[①] That was if they knew where the men had gone and how they could find them. And how would they be able to do that?

Liverpool MP Bessie Braddock asked questions in Parliament. There were no answers.[②] And we hear no more about the women, their protest or their fate. They disappear from the record.

10.1 A part of the community

We cannot get the exact numbers but we can get some indication of just how many people had had their lives damaged by the forced repatriations. The marriage records and christening records in Liverpool for the War years give us that. When we look at these we get the names of those affected. Where they lived. We see the names of their children. The churches they attended. The tragedy becomes more than numbers.

In 1942, with the Chinese seamen's strike over, Gabrielle Ellen Theresa Birkett applied to the Guardians of Infants to be allowed to marry Chun Hing. She was not yet 21 and needed her parents

① Article in 'News Chronicle', August 19th, 1946; File HO 213/926, National Archives, Kew.

② Note to file by S. E. Dudley. Dated August 27th, 1946; File HO 213/926, National Archives, Kew.

向并知道怎样找到男人，他们又能够怎样做呢?

利物浦议员贝西·布拉多克在议会上发起提案。但议会并没有答复。我们再也听不到关于女人、女人的抗议以及她们的命运的事情了。她们从历史的记录中消失了。

第一节　社区的一部分

那么到底有多少人的生活因强制遣返政策遭受破坏呢？虽然我们不能得到确切的数字，但是我们可以获取到一些线索。利物浦战争年代的结婚记录和洗礼记录可以给我们一些线索。当看到这些的时候，我们知道了那些受害者的名字，知道了她们曾在哪里居住，知道了她们孩子的名字，知道了孩子们接受洗礼的教堂。相比于数字，这些悲剧让人们更心痛。

1942 年，随着中国海员罢工结束，加布里埃尔·埃伦·特丽莎·伯其特向婴儿监护局提出申请，希望能得到与邢春结婚的许可。她还不满 21 岁，需要父母的同意才能结婚。罢工结束了，加布里埃尔可以和邢春一起安顿下来。她的父亲去世了，母亲不允许年纪尚小的加布里埃尔与她的中国爱人结婚。但监

permission to marry. The strike was over and they could now afford to settle down together. Her father was dead and her mother would not give permission for the under age Gabrielle to marry her Chinese sweetheart. The Guardians gave her permission.① Was she one of those whose husbands were forced out of the UK only a few short years later?

If we look at the records of the churches near the Liverpool waterfront where the Anglo-Chinese couples lived we find them having their children christened like any other member of Liverpool's society. On the very eve of the War, 20th August 1939, Frank and Clara Nam have their child, Elaine Elisabeth Lillian, christened at Saint Saviours Church in Faulkner Street. Frank is a seaman. They give their address as 134 Upper Huskisson Street. Three and a half years later Thomas and Annie Nam have their daughter Patricia Lillian christened at the same church. Thomas is a seaman. They live at 132 upper Huskisson Street. Next door to Frank and Clara.② Are Frank and Thomas brothers? Is Lillian, after whom both girls appear to be named, their grandmother? Are Frank and Thomas part of Liverpool's established Anglo-Chinese community? Or are they men who have settled in the city? Do they survive the War? If they do, are they forced out?

As the War runs into its fourth and fifth years we find

---

① Case No.92, Page 58 Ref 347. MAG 7/10. Guardianship of Infants Register 1942; Liverpool Central Library.

② Baptism forms, St Saviours Church, Faulkner Street, Toxteth, Liverpool, SAV283/2/4 ST SAV 1924-49; Liverpool Central Library.

护局许可她结婚。加布里埃尔是短短几年后丈夫就被强行赶出英国的女人中的一员吗？

如果我们查阅中英夫妇居住的利物浦滨海区附近的教堂记录，就会发现他们同利物浦社区中的其他成员一样，也带着孩子接受洗礼仪式。在战争前夕，1939 年 8 月 20 日，弗兰克和克拉拉·南有了他们的孩子伊莱恩·伊丽莎白·莉莲，伊莱恩在福克纳街的圣救世主教堂接受洗礼。弗兰克是一名海员。他们所提供给教堂的地址是上哈斯基森街 134 号。三年半后，托马斯和安妮·南有了他们的女儿帕特丽夏·莉莲，帕特丽夏在同一家教堂接受了洗礼。托马斯也是一名海员。他们居住在上哈斯基森街 132 号，住在弗兰克和克拉拉的隔壁。弗兰克和托马斯是兄弟吗？ 两个女儿的姓氏都是莉莲，难道她们的祖母是莉莲吗？弗兰克和托马斯是利物浦已形成的华人社区的一分子吗？或者他们已经在利物浦定居？战后他们存活下来了吗？如果活下来了，他们被强行赶出英国了吗？

在战争进行了四五年的时候，我们发现中英夫妇所生孩子的数量在不断增加。夫妇们把他们的孩子带到圣救世主教堂接受洗礼仪式。1944 年，埃莉诺·崔、大卫·姚、梅·曹、乔治·宋以及海伦娜·严都在圣救世主教堂接受了洗礼。他们的父亲有

increasing numbers of children are being born to Anglo-Chinese couples. Couples who take their children to their church, Saint Saviours, to have them christened. Eleanor Tsui, David Yoa, May Chao, George Sing and Helena Yen are all christened at Saint Saviours in 1944. Their fathers have Chinese names. They are merchant seamen. Their mothers seem to be local girls. In 1945 Allan Fong, Kenneth Wong, Carol Ying, Victor Chan, Anthony Hood, Eileen Chi and David Sing the brother of George, are taken to the church. 1946 sees another seven Anglo-Chinese children christened at Saint Saviours. 1947 sees only two christenings.① The men have gone. There are no husbands to father more children. As we look through the records of the churches in the area near the Mersey River where the seamen and their families lived, we see the same pattern. Births and christenings grow up to 1946 then dramatically fall. A picture of the destruction of a community.

The records seem to indicate that there must have been many more than 150 or even 300 women left behind. Married women, that is. But not all of the women married the men that they loved. Many, perhaps the majority, did not. Young women were advised by older women with Chinese partners not to marry. The risk was too great. For any woman who married a Chinese man lost her British citizenship. She too became an alien.

① Ibidem.

中文名字，是商船上的海员。他们的母亲似乎是当地的姑娘。1945 年，艾伦·方、肯尼思·王、卡罗·应、维克多·成、安东尼·胡德、艾琳·齐和乔治的兄弟大卫·宋被带到教堂。1946 年，我们发现另外 7 名中英混血的孩子在圣救世主教堂接受洗礼。1947 年，我们发现只有两名孩子接受了洗礼。因为中国海员们离开了，不再有丈夫可以孕育更多的孩子了。中国海员和他们的家人居住在默西河畔，我们查看了附近地区的教堂记录，发现情况如出一辙。出生人数和洗礼次数在 1946 年前在持续增加，之后就急剧下降，展现了华人社区衰落的景象。

这些记录似乎暗示着在利物浦一定有超过 150 名甚至 300 名女人被遗弃，而她们都是结了婚的女人。但并不是所有的女人都嫁给了自己心爱的男人。很多女人，也许是大多数女人都没有嫁给自己爱的人。年长一点的当地女人建议年轻的女人不要和中国男人结婚，因为风险太大了。与中国男人结婚的女人会失去其英国公民的身份，她也就成了外国人。

10.2 Stateless or Chinese?

A woman who married an alien, a foreigner, herself became a foreigner. It was the law. The law did not apply to British men who married foreign-born women. It only applied to women. British women who suffered the misfortune of falling in love with a foreigner. Women who, following the moral norms of the day, married the man they loved.

The law on which this discrimination was based was the 1870 Naturalisation Act. Reinforced by 1905 Aliens Act and further legislation in 1914, it meant that women not only lost their citizenship but could not apply to regain it unless their husbands died or they divorced.[①] They could then apply under Section 10(6) of the British Nationality Acts of 1914 and 1933. The public Records Office at Kew does contain examples of women seeking to regain their British nationality. Or rather, to be naturalised as British citizens as if they were foreigners – which, legally they were.[②] The women who appear in the files were generally well educated and from the higher social classes of what was then a highly stratified society. The working class women who married the Chinese seamen were not likely to have heard of this provision in the law. Nor, if they had heard of it, were they likely to have the means to pursue it. Safer not to get married. You stood to lose too

① Bhabha, Jacqueline and Shutter, Sue 'Women's Movement: Women Under Immigration, Nationality and Refugee Law', Trentham Books, Stoke-on-Trent, 1994, pp.17 – 19.

② File HO213/396 Aliens Department – Home Office: Married Women; National Archives, Kew.

第二节　是没有国籍还是中国人？

与外国人结婚的英国女人自己也成了外国人，这是法律规定。但这条法律不适用于和外籍女子结婚的英国男人，它只适用于英国女人。英国女人因与外国人相爱而遭遇不幸。女人们按照当时的道德规范，应该与她们爱的男人结婚。

这项具有歧视性的法案可以追溯到《1870 年归化法案》，而《1905 年外国人法案》以及 1914 年的其他法案更加深了这一歧视，这意味着一旦与外籍男人结婚，英国女人不仅失去了她们的公民身份，而且也不能申请重新获得公民身份，除非她们的丈夫去世了或是她们离婚了。之后她们可以根据《1914 年英国国籍和外国人身份法案》和《1933 年英国国籍和外国人身份法案》第 10（6）条申请重获公民身份。基尤区（英格兰东南部）的历史档案馆里有女人企图重新获得英国国籍的例子，更确切地说是女人像外国人一样加入英国国籍成为英国公民的例子，从法律的角度来说，她们就是外国人。文件中提到的女人通常受过良好的教育，来自较高的社会阶层，当时社会等级分化明显。嫁给中国海员的工薪阶层的女人不可能听说过法律中的这项条款。即使是她们听说过，也不可能找到办法来重新获得英国国籍。所以，女人不结婚更安全，因为如果结婚的话，她将会失去很多权利。

much if you did.

As aliens, women who had married foreigners had no automatic right to live in Britain. Along with their husbands, they had to report regularly to the police. Nor were her children British unless they had been born in the UK. If they had been born in Britain, the children had the right to remain but neither of their parents had that right. There were women in the Anglo-Chinese community who knew this and were already living under the burden of having to report to the police. Women whose movement was restricted. Who had no access to any government help should their husband die at sea. Little surprise then that many young women in World War Two decided not to marry their Chinese partners.

The situation had been changed somewhat as a result of the 1933 British Nationality Act. This allowed women to keep their British citizenship if they would otherwise become stateless.[①] but, of course, China had an administration recognised by the British-The Nationalists led by Chiang kai-shek. The women were, therefore, Chinese.

This meant that women who married Chinese and had to travel did so on Chinese documents. So we see Olive Chan, born in Manchester in 1901 is recorded in Australia's immigration records in 1949 as being of 'Chinese nationality'.[②] Her photograph

① Bhabha, Jacqueline and Shutter, Sue 'Women's Movement: Women Under Immigration, Nationality and Refugee Law', Trentham Books, Stoke-on-Trent, 1994, p.24.

② File 1949/1003 Series A432/82, Australian National Archives, Canberra, Australia.

嫁给外国人的英国女人成了外国人，也就没有权利随意住在英国。她们需要和丈夫一起定期向警方报到。她们的孩子也不是英国人，除非孩子是在英国出生的。如果孩子在英国出生，那么孩子有权利留下来，但孩子的父母没有这种权利。华人社区的女人知道这一点，她们已经生活在向警局报到的压力下了。女人的行动受到限制，万一她们的丈夫在海上去世，她们得不到政府的任何帮助。所以“二战”期间很多年轻的女人决定不和她们的中国男友结婚也就不足为奇了。

《1933 年英国国籍和外国人身份法案》的出台，使得这一情况似乎有所改观。法案规定，如果她们与外籍男人结婚后没有国籍，允许她们保留英国国籍。但英国当然承认中国当时的政府，也就是蒋介石领导的国民政府。因此这些女人婚后在法律上是中国人。

这意味着英国女人嫁给中国人后，在旅行时不得不揣着中国的证明文件。所以我们发现 1901 年出生在曼彻斯特的奥利芙・陈作为拥有中国国籍的人出现在 1949 年的澳大利亚移民记录中。她的资料上附带着她的照片。从外表上看奥利芙完全是白种人，但她和一个中国男人结了婚，因此她也成了中国人。

accompanies her papers. She is totally Caucasian in appearance but she was married to a Chinese man. Therefore, she was Chinese.

Why she was travelling to Australia we do not know. But if she and her Chinese husband sought to escape the restrictions on them in the UK and emigrate so they could be together, she would certainly not get into Australia. That country may have been avidly recruiting people for its vast empty land, but it certainly did not want yellow ones. Anyway, it too was attempting to get rid of the Chinese seamen who had been sailing for British-owned companies and who had attempted to settle in the country.

Such was Australia's determination to rid the country of the Chinese that it had passed a law to get rid of them and any other Asians who had been given refuge in the country during the War. The War-time Refugees Removal Bill had it's second reading on June 1st 1949 and Arthur Calwell, the Minister for Immigration, made it clear that marriage to an Australian woman by an Asian man should not be regarded as '...ground for authorizing his permanent admission.'[①] The Chinese had to go and their wives would not be allowed to go with them.[②]

Eventually, the Australian attempt to force the Chinese mariners out of the country failed. In 1950 an appeal by 38 of the men married to Australian women was upheld. His Honor Mr. Justice Williams judged that a deportation order against men who

① File A 4968 25/10/2, Australian National Archives, Canberra, Australia.

② Paper presented by Sir Frank Eggleston, May 12th, 1949,File A 4968 25/10/2, Australian National Archives, Canberra, Australia.

至于奥利芙为什么去澳大利亚，我们不得而知。但如果她和她的中国丈夫是企图逃避英国对他们施加的一些限制而进行移民，从而达到在一起的目的，那么她一定不该去澳大利亚。澳大利亚由于其广阔的空地，也许一直在急切地招人，但这个国家一定不想要黄种人。总之，澳大利亚也在尝试着清除当地为英国公司当船员的中国海员，以及那些想要定居在此的中国海员。

澳大利亚下定决心将境内的中国人赶走，因此颁布了法令来驱逐中国人以及其他任何战争期间在澳大利亚避难的亚洲人。1949 年 6 月 1 日，《战时难民遣返法案》被二次宣读，移民部部长亚瑟·卡尔韦尔明确表示与澳大利亚女人结婚的亚洲男人不应该被视为“有理由得到政府的永久接纳”。中国人不得不离开，而且澳大利亚不允许他们的妻子与他们一同离开。

然而，最终澳大利亚强行驱逐中国海员的尝试失败了。1950 年，38 名与澳大利亚女人结婚的中国男人提出上诉，得到了法院的支持。国王陛下的威廉大法官判定对“已经成为澳大利亚社会成员的”中国人实施的放逐令是无效的。中国人终于可以和他们的妻子重新团圆了。

'...have become members of the Australian community...' was not valid.[1] The men could be re-united with their wives.

Not so in Britain. The men would not be able to come back, as we shall see. The women would have to wait to get to become British citizens again. In 1948 the British Nationality Act gave citizenship to all those born in the UK's colonies. British women who married foreign men were able to retain their British nationality unless they decided to give it up. The era of mass migration into the UK had arrived.

For the women torn apart from their Chinese husbands this helped not at all. The men had gone. As you will see in the case studies, those who were Catholics could not re-marry until the Church recognised that their marriages were over and that would be many years into the future. For those who had never married, the new law was an irrelevance. Married or unmarried, the women and their children now faced a nightmare of poverty and deprivation.

What did those women who had left with their husbands face when they go to Hong Kong, to Singapore or to China? Hong Kong and Singapore had been shattered by the war. But they would recover. And the men who had been forced to leave their families might be able to get back to Britain. For those couples who had gone to China a bleak future awaited them. For the men who had gone back alone, the possibility of returning was soon to be diminishingly small.

---

① Judgement before His Honour Mr Justice Williams, Sydney, Wednesday May 24th, 1950 at 10：30 AM, File 1949/1003 Series A432/82, Australian National Archives, Canberra, Australia.

但在英国不是这样。正如我们看到的那样，中国男人再也不能回到英国了。他们的英国妻子需要等待着重新得到英国公民的身份。《1948 年英国国籍法案》赋予所有在英国殖民地出生的人公民身份。与外国男人结婚的英国女人能够保留她们的英国国籍，除非她们决定放弃国籍。大批移民迁入英国的时代到来了。

对于那些和中国丈夫分离的英国女人来说，这根本不起作用。首先，她们的男人已经走了；其次，这些身为天主教教徒的英国女人只有在教堂承认她们的婚姻结束后才能再婚，而这在未来很多年后才能成为现实。对于那些未婚有子的英国女人来说，新法律无关紧要。无论是否结婚，女人和她们的孩子现在都面临着贫穷和困苦的噩梦。

那些随着丈夫离开的女人去香港、新加坡或者中国大陆后会面临什么样的状况呢？香港和新加坡虽然已经被战争摧毁，但它们会重新恢复，而且去了香港和新加坡的那些夫妇也许可以回到英国。对于那些已经去了中国大陆的夫妇来说，未来一片黯淡。对于独自回国的中国人来说，回到英国的可能性越来越小。

11

Chapter 11. Back home

第十一章　回家

As Fred Bishop had learned, for many of the men being forced out of Britain their 'home' was in the UK. It was not Singapore, Hong Kong or China. It was now Liverpool. But they had been given no choice. They had to go back.

For men working for Anglo-Saxon Petroleum 'home' had often been Singapore. An island where the infrastructure had been run down by the Japanese occupiers and goods of any kind were scarce in the extreme. So many people had lost such property as they had owned. It had been destroyed during the battle for the city or the years of occupation that followed; but life had to go on. The British administration was back and it had been welcomed with relief. As Lee Kuan Yew the future Prime Minister of an independent Singapore wrote in his memoirs, the British soldiers '...reciprocated the warm we showed them and ...shared their... rations...with the people ....'[①] An experience that contrasted all too sharply with the treatment the returned mariners had so recently experienced in the troops' homeland. The homeland for which those seamen had been risking their lives and from which they had now been expelled.

Lee Kuan Yew would leave for Cambridge University in September 1946 to study law – just as the last of the Singapore seamen were finishing their journey in the opposite direction. He would gain a Double First at that prestigious seat of learning and go on to lead Singapore to independence and prosperity. There

① Lee, Kuan Yew, The Singapore Story: Memoirs of Lee Kuan Yew, Prentice Hall, Singapore, 1998, p.86.

正如弗雷德·毕晓普所了解的，对很多被赶出英国的中国人来说，他们的“家”在英国，而不在新加坡、香港或中国大陆。而现在他们别无选择，不得不回去。

对于为壳牌石油公司工作的中国海员来说，新加坡常常是他们的“家”。日本占领者毁坏了这座岛的基础设施，各种商品都极度短缺，很多人失去了财产。新加坡在城市争夺战中遭到摧毁，接下来日本人数年的殖民也在摧毁着这座城。但人们的生活还得继续。之后英国政府又开始接管新加坡，当地人心怀慰藉地欢迎。后来新加坡成为独立的国家，正如其将来的总理李光耀在他的回忆录中所写：英国士兵对我们所表示的友好予以回报，与人民分享他们的口粮。英国士兵在新加坡享有的友好和中国海员遭受的待遇形成非常鲜明的对比。这些海员曾经一直为了他们心中的“家”拿生命冒险，现在他们却要从这里被赶走。

李光耀在 1946 年 9 月前往剑桥大学学习法律，这时最后一批新加坡海员刚从英国回到新加坡，结束了他们的航行。李光耀将在著名高等学府得到双科优等的成绩，继而领导新加坡走向独立和繁荣。“狮城”在前进的道路上也许会面临困难，然而未来是光明的。但我们永远不知道那些在新加坡的中国海员所感受到的痛苦，他们曾被迫离开在英格兰的家人，如今又

would be struggles ahead for the Lion City, nevertheless the future was bright. But we will never know the anguish felt by those Singapore men who had been forced to leave their families back in England.

Hong Kong had suffered just as badly under the Japanese. The port had been wrecked by Japanese neglect① and the heavy bombing carried out by the Americans. The country to which Britain was now heavily indebted and whose government had been pressuring the British to hand the colony over to Chiang Kai Shek.② Given what was now happening in China and what was to follow in the years ahead, perhaps the gods were now smiling on Fragrant Harbour. Churchill had ordered units of the British Pacific fleet to get there before the Americans. They did so. On 30th August 1945 they took the Japanese surrender. Hong Kong would remain under British administration until 1997.

Butterfield and Swire, Holt's agents in the territory, were now assessing the company's losses. They could only find one of the vessels that Holt had owned before the War. The rest had disappeared – sunk, stolen or simply destroyed. Key personnel had died in Japanese captivity or like Holt's ships, had disappeared.③

① Report HQ Port Commandant, Kowloon, Hong Kong, October 20th, 1945 'Report on Rehabilitation of the Port of Kowloon-Hong Kong on Short and Long Term Policy' by C. R. Janvrin, Major, Port Commander; File 7D 1121, Ocean Archive, Liverpool Maritime Museum.

② Endacott, G. B 'A History of Hong Kong', Oxford in Asia, Oxford University Press, Hong Kong, 1964.

③ Letter from Butterfield and Swire, Hong Kong to Alfred Holt and Company, Liverpool, September 11th, 1945; File 7D 1121, Ocean Archive, Liverpool Maritime Museum, UK. Letter from Butterfield and Swire, Hong Kong to Alfred Holt and Company, Liverpool, October 31st, 1945; File 7D 1121, Ocean Archive, Liverpool Maritime Museum.

要被新加坡驱逐回去。

香港也在日本人的侵占下饱受重创。港口设施因日本人的忽视及美国人的狂轰滥炸而遭到毁坏。美国政府一直对欠其巨额债务的英国施加压力，要求英国向蒋介石交出香港殖民地。与苦难的中国大陆不同，香港也许受到了老天的恩泽。丘吉尔命令英国太平洋舰队的部队在美军之前抵达香港，而他们也做到了。1945 年 8 月 30 日，他们在香港接受日军投降。直到 1997 年，香港一直在英国政府的管理之下。

太古轮船公司是霍尔特在这一区域的代理，他们正在评估公司的损失。他们只找到了霍尔特战前所拥有的船只中的一艘。其余的船都不见了，有的沉入大海，有的被人偷走或者被摧毁了。船上重要的工作人员或者被日本俘虏后死去，或者失踪消失不见。很多人被日本人强迫去往中国大陆。他们也许已经去世，或者在内战中被抓了起来。内战又一次在摧残这个不幸的国家。

Inevitably, many would have been forced by the Japanese to go to China. They too may have died or were now caught up in the civil war that was again raging in that sad country.

11.1 Chaos, corruption and violence

China had lost three million soldiers killed. Countless more had been wounded. Fifteen to twenty million civilians had died. Nobody knew even approximately how many. Both urban and rural society were fractured. Tens of millions were homeless and wandering the country. Families had been separated and many of the returning seamen would never find their kin. Communities had been split asunder as the war was fought over their villages and towns. The social cohesion that was the bedrock on which the Confucian social system had been built was shattered. The widows, the orphans, the millions of wounded and injured had no government or social net to support them.[①]

In a land without an effective road network, the railways no longer ran. The modern economy, such as it was, was broken and no longer operated. Inflation was rocketing to ever-dizzier heights. The Wholesale Price Index for Shanghai tells the story. Taking May 1937 as the base, prices had risen 16-fold by December 1941. By December 1945 they were over 177,000 times their level in 1937. By December 1947 nearly 17 million times their pre-

① Lary, Diana 'China's Republic', Cambridge University Press, New York, 2007, pp.159 – 164.

第一节 混乱、腐败以及暴力

“二战”导致300万名中国士兵战死沙场，无数的人受了伤。大约1500万到2000万的老百姓丧生，没有人知道伤亡人数具体是多少。城市和乡村都遭到破坏。千百万人无家可归，流离失所，很多回乡的海员也许永远找不到他们的亲人。随着战争在村庄和城镇打响，人们生活的村镇四分五裂。建立在和谐基础上的儒家社会制度土崩瓦解。寡妇、孤儿以及无数受伤的人得不到政府或社会机构的保障。

由于没有有效的陆路交通网，铁路也无法运行。现代经济支离破碎，并且不再发展。物价迅速上涨，通货膨胀达到了前所未有的严重程度。上海的批发物价指数足以说明一切。以1937年5月的物价为基准，到1941年12月，物价已经上涨16倍。到了1945年12月，物价比1937年上涨超过17.7万倍。到了1947年12月，差不多比战前的物价水平上涨1700万倍。1948年12月，上涨倍数达到了令人难以理解的367.88亿倍。实际上，钱根本一文不值。1949年4月，国民党政府倒台时，

war level. December 1948 the figure was an incomprehensible 36,788,000,000. Money was, in effect, totally worthless. April 1949 and the collapse of the Nationalist Government saw the index at 151,733,000,000,000. Money was quite literally not worth the paper on which it was printed.①

Corruption, the corrosive acid that seems to forever eat away at Chinese society, was rampant. In Shanghai United Nations relief supplies were being plundered and sold on the black market.② Nationalist officials and gangsters profited. The people starved and the violence did not end. With the Japanese gone, the Nationalists and the Communists were at each other's throats and the population were caught in the middle.

The Communists were now active in Shanghai. The Party would have tried to protect those of the seaman who had been active in the Communist Liverpool Chinese Seamen's Union on their return to Shanghai. Were they now part of this Communist underground movement? Had they survived? Fred Bishop had seen uniformed men waiting for the seamen as they disembarked in Shanghai. Unionists were being arrested. The Nationalists were murdering and torturing anyone they suspected of Communist or even social-democratic sympathies.③ As a UK trade mission to China in 1946 noted, those who were politically active were '...apt

① Chou, Shun-Hsin 'The Chinese Inflation 1937-1949', Columbia University Press, New York, 1963, p.248.

② Rowan, Roy 'Chasing the Dragon', The Lyons Press, Guilford, Connecticut, 2004, p.30.

③ Letter from the Acting Secretary-General, TUC, August 28th, 1946 to Mr Tewson of the Foreign Office; File FO 371/53679; National Archives, Kew, UK.

上涨倍数达到 151.733 万亿倍。纸币都没有印钱的纸值钱。

腐败如同腐蚀性酸液一般一直在吞噬着中国社会，蔓延在这片土地上。在上海，联合国的善后救济物资被大肆洗劫，然后在黑市上售卖。国民党官员和黑帮沆瀣一气从中获利。老百姓忍饥挨饿的同时，还要面对不断恶化的社会治安问题。随着日本人的投降，国民党和共产党势如水火，内战再一次给人民带来了苦难。

日本投降后，中国共产党在上海的活动又活跃了起来。共产党试图保护那些在利物浦由共产党领导的在工会中表现活跃的中国海员，此时他们正在返回上海的途中。他们现在是共产党地下活动的参与者了吗？他们存活下来了吗？弗雷德·毕晓普看到国民党军人等待着在上海登陆的海员。海员工会的成员遭到逮捕。国民党杀害并折磨着任何一个他们怀疑是共产党的人，甚至连拥护社会民主的人也不放过。1946 年英国派往中国的贸易代表团记录：那些在政治上活跃的人“很容易就消失了”。但那些不活跃的中国共产党人怎么样了呢？

to disappear...'① But what of those who were not active members of the Chinese Communist Party?

Papers in the Shanghai Municipal Archives give us an insight into what happened to all too many of the men. From their correspondence, we can hear their voices. Voices that became increasingly desperate as time wore on. Li Jan Hai registered with the Nationalist Chinese Seamen's Union in Shanghai on October 24th, 1945 hoping they could help him to find work. Six months later he wrote to Councillor Zhang Yao Ming of the Union. He had heard nothing 'It seems the CSU has forgotten me.' His family are finding it difficult to survive.② He was not alone. Even when men do find work, they are not being paid. The so-called Princely Hong, the firm of Jardine, is not paying wages they owe. Neither is the American company Texaco.

The Nationalist Chinese Seamen's Union had moved from Liverpool to Shanghai at the end of September 1945.③ But even with the support of the Nationalist Government it could do little to help the men. In April 1946 men who have returned from the UK have still found no work. They are trapped in boarding houses in the city without money and without hope of employment.④

① Note to file by Peggy Cripps (daughter of Sir Stafford Cripps and part of the UK Trade Mission to China), dated 18.11.46; File 951/1, Modern Records Centre, University of Warwick, UK.

② Letter from Li Jan Hai to Councillor Zhang Yao Ming, Chinese Seamen's Union, Shanghai, File QF 164-2-77; Shanghai Municipal Archives, People's Republic of China.

③ Note on File Q 199-42-47, 1947-1950; Shanghai Municipal Archives.

④ Report from No. 1 Temporary Boarding House, April 15th, 1946; File QF 164-2-77; Shanghai Municipal Archives, People's Republic of China.

上海市档案馆的文件让我们了解到发生在很多共产党人身上的事情。从他们的信函中，我们可以听到他们的呼声。随着时间的推移，呼声变得越来越绝望。1945 年 10 月 24 日，李建海在上海的国民党中国海员工会登记，希望他们能帮助他找到工作。六个月后，他又给工会委员张耀明写信。但他始终也没有得到任何答复，他觉得“似乎工会遗忘我了”。他的家人发现难以生存下去了。不止李建海一个人这样，甚至那些已经找到工作的人也没有得到报酬。怡和洋行，也就是所谓的“高贵的香港公司”拒绝支付他们所拖欠的薪资。美国的德士古公司也没有付给员工薪水。

1945 年 9 月底，国民党控制的中国海员工会从利物浦搬到了上海，但即使是得到了国民党政府的支持，工会依然帮不上这些海员。1946 年 4 月，从英国回来的海员依旧找不到工作。他们被困在寄宿公寓里，没有钱，也没有找到工作的希望。工会继续与南京的国民党交通运输部讨论应该采取的措施。他们想帮助海员找工作，但是最终什么也没做。

Discussions on what can be done go on between the Union and the Nationalist Transport Department in Nanjing. They will help the men find work.① Nothing happens.

Men who had lost their jobs when they got back to China try to help themselves. Possibly these are the men that Holt was determined to purge from its fleet. They form an Association for Seamen Who Came Back from Overseas headed by Hao Shi Qing. They ask for help from the Union in getting jobs with China Merchants fleet, the shipping line owned by the Chinese Government. As we shall see from the case studies telling the stories of the families of the men, it seems that some may have been able to get work.②

Even when the men do find work, they are cheated and exploited. Mobil and Shell recruit 400 men through a contractor, Zhu Quan Hong. The men are to be paid $85 a month but $20 of this goes to Zhu who also charges the men an 'agency fee' of $32.50. He makes $13,000 from the transaction. Presumably this is US dollars since, by this time, the Chinese currency is well on its way to being worthless.③

Desperate men would be unlikely to argue. And by now men

① 'Official Document' China Merchants Department, April 1st, 1946, File QF 164-2-77; Shanghai Municipal Archives, People's Republic of China.

② Letter from Hao Shi Qing of the Association for Seamen who Came Back from Overseas' to Chinese Seamen's Union, Shanghai, April, 1946; File Q164-3-32, Shanghai Municipal Archives, People's Republic of China.

③ Report by the Social Department of the Chinese Seamen's Union; File Q6-7-75 January 11, 1946 to February 19, 1946; Shanghai Municipal Archives, People's Republic of China.

这些回到中国时失去工作的海员们试图自力更生。也许这些海员就是从霍尔特公司的船上被迫离开的人。他们成立了海归海员协会，领导者是郝释清。他们向工会寻求帮助，希望能在中国政府的轮船公司——国营轮船招商局的船队上找到工作。正如我们在一些讲述海员家人们故事的研究案例中所见，有些海员似乎找到了工作。

即使海员们找到了工作，他们还是遭到欺骗和剥削。美孚石油公司和壳牌公司在包工头朱全红的介绍下雇佣了 400 名海员。海员们每个月本应该得到 85 美元的薪水，但其中的 20 美元却进入朱的口袋，而且朱还向海员们收取 32.5 美元的“中介费”。他通过这笔交易赚了 1.3 万美元。那时朱赚的是美元，大概就是从这个时候开始，中国货币逐渐变得一文不值。

绝望的人们不可能去争论薪水的高低，而且人们现在依旧很绝望。宋杰为壳牌公司工作。当新加坡沦陷落入日本人手中时，他设法成功逃到了印度。“二战”过后，宋杰回到上海，他失去了工作。当时，像霍尔特这样的公司正在广东省雇佣更廉价的劳动力。他写信给工会，请求他们帮助他找到工作。这时已经是 1946 年 8 月，自从宋杰回国后就一直没找到工作。

are desperate. Song Jie had worked for Shell. When Singapore was lost to the Japanese, he managed to escape to India. After the War, he went back to Shanghai. He lost his job. The company, like Holt was hiring cheaper labour in Guangdong Province. He writes to the Union asking them to help him find work. It is August 1946 and he has not worked since his return.①

The years 1947 and 1948 show little improvement. The Union writes to shipping companies trying to get work for the men. They try China Merchants again. The company has bought a lot of new ships. The Union has many, many experienced mariners on its books, men who have sailed with Holt, with Jardine and with Texaco.② By the beginning of 1949, when the Nationalists are on the point of losing the civil war, the Union is writing to the Foreign Affairs Ministry in Shanghai that unemployment is still high amongst '...men who returned from abroad after the War.' It provides a list of some of the men who have still not found work three and a half years after the War's end.③

11.2 The blacklist

How many of these men were amongst the 'troublemakers' that

① Letter from Song Jie to Chinese Seamen's Union, August 6th, 1946; File Q164-4-35; Shanghai Municipal Archives, People's Republic of China.

② Letters in File Q164-2-28 Chinese Seamen's Union, Shanghai Branch August 1947-September 1948; Shanghai Municipal Archives, People's Republic of China.

③ Letter from Chinese Seamen's Union, Shanghai Branch to Foreign Affairs Ministry, Shanghai, File Q164-2-28 November 1948 to January 1948; Shanghai Municipal Archives, People's Republic of China.

1947 年和 1948 年，情况没有什么好转。工会给船运公司写信，试图为这些人找到工作。他们又一次试着联系轮船招商局，因为招商局购买了许多艘新船。工会有很多有经验的海员，他们的名字登记在工会簿上，这些人曾为霍尔特、怡和、德士古等公司工作。到了 1949 年年初，当国民党在内战中正处于失利地位时，工会给上海的外交部写信，信中说“‘二战’后从国外回来的海员们的失业率依旧很高”。工会提供了一份名单，其中，有的海员在“二战”结束三年半后依旧没有找到工作。

第二节　黑名单

这些人中有多少曾是霍尔特急于肃清的“制造麻烦的人”？又有多少曾是离开他们利物浦的家人被迫回国的人？

Holt had been so anxious to purge? How many had left families in Liverpool?

With the encouragement of the British Government, Holt operated a blacklist of so-called left-wing agitators after the War.① The union activists involved in organising the Chinese mariners. Whether these men had family in the UK or not, these would have been the men that Holt focused on. Holt and the British Government wanted these men out of the country. And they wanted them kept out.

There is one particularly striking piece of evidence that helps support the argument that the unemployed seamen had been blacklisted. Amongst them may have been Hao Shi Qing and the men of his Association. By 1947 Holt was having trouble recruiting fitters, bosuns and other skilled men in Shanghai. They had cut their rates so low at the end of the War that men would not join them. Even after increasing their rates by 50% in 1947, they were still experiencing difficulties.② And yet so many experienced men could not find work. How could this be unless these were the men that Holt would not employ?

11.3 Where are the men?

At the War's end the Communist Liverpool Chinese Seamen's

① File CAB, National Archives, Kew, UK. Cited by Benton, G and Gomez, T in 'The Chinese in Britain 1800 – Present', Chapter 3. Pre-publication copy sent to the authors.

② Note to file: Conversation with Mr H. E. Price, File 951/1 2A , Chinese Crews 1945-1955, Ocean Archive, Liverpool Maritime Museum, UK.

在英国政府的鼓励下，霍尔特公司在战后列出一份所谓左翼煽动分子的黑名单。这些参与组织中国海员工会的积极分子，无论他们在英国有没有家庭，他们都是霍尔特所针对的对象。霍尔特和英国政府想要把这些人赶出英国，他们要让这些人待在英国境外。

一项非常惊人的证据印证了这一论断，即那些没有找到工作的海员都是黑名单上的人。这些人中也许有郝释清及其协会的成员。到了 1947 年，霍尔特在上海雇佣修理工、水手长以及其他的一些技术人员时遇到了困难。因为在战争快结束时，霍尔特公司把员工的薪资降得非常低，以至于员工们不愿意加入其公司。1947 年，即使将员工的薪资上涨了 50% 之后，他们依旧招募困难，但是，太多富有经验的海员仍然没有找到工作。怎么可能出现这种情况呢？除非这些人就是霍尔特不能雇佣的黑名单里的人。

第三节　海员们在哪里？

战争快结束时，共产党控制的利物浦中国海员工会整体搬迁到了香港。在这里，工会人员可以保证自身的安全，不受到国民党的迫害。这里足够安全，工会人员重新成立了香港海员工会，并在其中任职。今天，香港海员工会依然在发挥着作用，

Union had moved '... lock, stock and barrel...' to Hong Kong.[1] There its officials would be safe from the Nationalists. Safe to reestablish the Hong Kong Seamen's Union and to metamorphose themselves into officials of that union. Today the Union still operates. It is still in Jordan Road, Kowloon close to the old waterfront. Sadly, its present-day officials have scant knowledge of its history and its records reveal little. But the Holt archives show that shortly after the War, Holt officials found themselves meeting yet again the same men they had negotiated with during the War years. Men such as Pong Kam Yau who had been the Chairman of the Liverpool Union from 1942 to 1946. Leung Chuen who had been an employee of Holt and had been an Executive Official in Liverpool was now in more or less the same position in the Hong Kong Union. And so was Shum Wai – another ex-Holt man and Executive of the Liverpool Union.

If the Union officials were able to set up shop in Hong Kong, how many other men from Shanghai were able to do the same? We know that Shanghai men were being held in Hong Kong at the beginning of 1946 because there were so few ships going beyond Singapore at that time. Men were also on shore in Singapore for similar reasons.[2] Conversations with now elderly Chinese seamen confirm that men did jump ship in each of these ports. Perhaps they

---

① Ibidem.

② Letter from Butterfield and Swire, Hong Kong and Singapore to Alfred Holt and Company, Liverpool, March 15th, 1946; File 2342 2A, Chinese Crews 1945 – 1955, Ocean Archive, Liverpool Maritime Museum, UK.

依然位于距离老滨海区很近的九龙佐敦道上。然而，令人感到悲哀的是，工会现在的工作人员对于工会的历史所知甚少，而且工会的记录资料也没有反映出当时的具体信息。但霍尔特公司的档案显示，战争结束后不久，霍尔特的工作人员再一次见到了他们在战争年代曾与之谈判的中国海员。例如在 1942 年至 1946 年间担任利物浦工会主席的彭锦有；曾经是霍尔特公司的海员并曾在利物浦工会担任行政人员的梁春，而且梁春现在还在香港工会担任类似的职位；另外还有岑维，岑维之前也是霍尔特公司的海员，并担任利物浦工会的执行委员。

如果工会的工作人员能够在香港开设商店的话，那么有多少从上海来的其他海员也可以这样做呢？我们知道 1946 年年初时上海海员被滞留在香港，因为当时目的地比新加坡更远的地方的船只太少了。海员们也因为同样的原因在新加坡岸上滞留。与现在年长的中国海员之间的谈话也证实了在这些港口都有海员跳船。[①] 也许他们希望尝试着回到利物浦家人的身边。也许他们在英国没有家人，但他们渴望逃离饱受战争摧残的中国大陆。

① 即海员到达港口后，从船上逃走，不再上船工作。——译者注

wished to try to get back to their families in Liverpool. Perhaps they had no families in Britain but were anxious to avoid returning to strife–torn China.

From the evidence available to us, it seems that Hong Kong men had gone back to Hong Kong. Singapore men to Singapore. But Shanghai men were now in Hong Kong and Singapore as well as Shanghai. Possibly some of the men who had been blacklisted by Holt got jobs with the Nationalist owned China Merchants. This was possible if they had no traceable record of involvement in the Communist Union in Liverpool. Possibly they changed identity buying the papers of men who had not been blacklisted. Interviews with old seamen show that this was not unknown. When Shanghai fell to the Communists, did they end up in Taiwan? As the case studies show, that this may have happened to some of the men forced to leave their families in Liverpool.

And some were sailing south to Hong Kong in ships owned by Shanghai ship owners to add to the numbers already in the British colony.① In Shanghai itself the situation was deteriorating fast. Rice was unobtainable, flour was rationed and being doled out to Shanghai citizens, there were riots at the food stores.② Soon Nationalist troops were trying to commandeer ships to escape from

① Letter from Butterfield and Swire, Shanghai to Alfred Holt and Company, Liverpool, December 3rd, 1948; File 7D 1148 Shanghai Situation 1945/48/49/50, Ocean Archive, Liverpool Maritime Museum, UK.

② Letter headed from Butterfield and Swire, Shanghai to Alfred Holt and Company, Liverpool, November 12th, 1948; File 7D 1148 Shanghai Situation 1945/48/49/50, Ocean Archive, Liverpool Maritime Museum, UK.

从我们得到的证据来看，香港海员似乎已经回到了香港，新加坡海员也回到了新加坡，但有的上海海员现在还在香港和新加坡，只有少部分回到了上海。霍尔特黑名单上的一些海员也许在国民党的轮船招商局找到了工作，但前提是他们没有参与共产党领导的利物浦海员工会的可追踪记录。他们也可能通过购买那些没有列入黑名单的海员的证件而改变了身份。年老的海员在采访中表示有这样的事情发生。当上海解放时，他们去了台湾吗？正如一些案例研究表明，一些被迫离开他们利物浦家人的海员也许经历了这些变故。

一些海员乘坐上海船东的船南行至香港，加入已经在英国殖民地的人当中。上海的情况很快变得越来越糟。大米无法获取，面粉定量供应，以小份发放给上海的市民。食品商店发生骚乱。不久国民党军队尝试着征用船只逃跑，来躲避距离他们越来越近的共产党军队。到了 1949 年 4 月，共产党军队距离上海只有 50 公里。所谓的共产党员被游街示众，之后被枪毙，或是被国民党带进法租界闲置的房屋内，遭受折磨，然后被枪杀。1949 年 5 月 24 日，中国人民解放军进入法租界。上海的内战自此结束。

the approaching Communist army①. By April 1949 that army was only 50 miles from Shanghai.② Alleged Communists were being paraded through town before being shot or taken to an abandoned house in the French Concession, tortured and then shot③. The People's Liberation Army entered the French Concession on 24th May 1949. For Shanghai, the civil war was over.

Soon, the Nationalists were blockading the port. Travel restrictions were imposed by the new Communist regime.④ The seamen who have not already escaped to Taiwan or Hong Kong were trapped. China would not open up to the outside world again for thirty years. There would be no return for them to their families in Liverpool.

① Letter headed from Butterfield and Swire, Shanghai to Alfred Holt and Company, Liverpool, December 18th, 1948; File 7D 1148 Shanghai Situation 1945/48/49/50, Ocean Archive, Liverpool Maritime Museum, UK.

② Letter headed from Butterfield and Swire, Shanghai to Alfred Holt and Company, Liverpool, April 29th, 1949; File 7D 1148 Shanghai Situation 1945/48/49/50, Ocean Archive, Liverpool Maritime Museum, UK.

③ Fenby, J 'Modern China: the Fall and Rise of a Great Power, 1850 to the present', HarperCollins, New York, 2008, p.348.

④ Letter headed from Butterfield and Swire, Shanghai to Alfred Holt and Company, Liverpool, June 8th, 1950; File 7D 1148 Shanghai Situation 1945/48/49/50, Ocean Archive, Liverpool Maritime Museum, UK.

国民党不久后就封锁了港口。新上任的共产党政权，为了维护稳定，也强制实施了人口流动限制措施。那些还没有去往台湾或香港地区的海员被困了起来。中国在之后的三十年里一直没有对外开放，因此中国海员无法回到他们的利物浦亲人的身边。

12

Chapter 12. Why?

第十二章　原因何在？

12.1 Bankrupt

The Britain that the men had left was bankrupt. She had focused all her efforts on winning the War and had destroyed her economy in the process.①

The ships on which the Chinese mariners had been sailing had brought the tools of war. Little had been exported to pay for those vital supplies. By 1944 Britain's exports paid for no more than 1% of her imports.② From 1941 onwards she had been earning a miniscule $100,000 a year from her exports. The saviour had been President Roosevelt of the United States. When Britain's investments had all been sold to pay for her imports, the Americans had kept Britain alive. They had done it with Lend–Lease under which they had leased or lent Britain what she had needed to fight. Thirty billion of the fifty billion dollars Britain had spent had come via Lend-Lease. One fifth of the food Britons ate now came from the USA, paid for by Lend-Lease.③

Now the War was over and Roosevelt was dead. The Japanese had surrendered on 15th August 1945 and one week later America's new leader, President Truman, had ended Lend-Lease. Britain was now in the position where she did not have enough dollars to purchase the food she needed to feed her population.

① Marr, A 'A History of Modern Britain', Pan Macmillan, London, 2008, p.10.

② Clarke, P 'The Last Thousand Days of the British Empire', Bloomsbury Press, New York, 2008, p28.

③ Marr, A 'A History of Modern Britain', Pan Macmillan, London, 2008, p.10.

第一节　破产

迫使中国海员离开的英国破产了。英国把全部的精力都放在了赢取战争的胜利上,而这一过程也摧毁了英国本国的经济。

中国海员曾经工作过的轮船被用于运输战争物资。由于其出口的货物很少，利润都不足以支付这些重要的战争物资。到1944年时,英国出口所赚的利润只够付其进口货物1%的费用。从1941年开始,英国通过出口货物只赚取了极少的10万美元。美国总统罗斯福成了英国的救星。英国通过售卖资产来支付其进口商品的费用，这时美国人带给英国一线生机。美国人通过了《租借法案》，他们按照法案出租或者借给英国打仗所需的东西。英国战争期间花费的500亿美元中有300亿美元是通过《租借法案》获得的。英国人所食用的五分之一的食物也是来自美国，也是通过《租借法案》得来的。

现在战争结束了，罗斯福总统也已经逝世。1945年8月15日，日本人宣布投降，一个星期之后，美国的新任领袖杜鲁门总统终止了《租借法案》。英国陷入了这样的一种境况，即国库没有足够的美元来购买供英国百姓果腹的食物。

The wartime trans-Atlantic alliance was over and both countries now had new leaders. Scarcely one month before Truman cut Britain's lifeline, the Labour Party under Clement Attlee had won a landslide victory. The party had pledged to implement a raft of new and costly policies faced a crisis. One that would continue throughout their time in government. The country was effectively bankrupt yet over the next eighteen months four million men would leave the armed services; they had to have work.[①] These men and their families had to have somewhere to live, but there was an acute housing shortage. One that was especially bad in cities like London and Liverpool, which had been so heavily bombed.

The new Labour Government sent the greatest economist of the age, Lord Keynes, to negotiate with the Americans. In reality, he went with a begging bowl hoping that Britain's wartime ally and financial benefactor would continue its generosity. Keynes wanted a $6 billion interest free loan. But the old relationship had died with Roosevelt. The Americans did not know just how broke Britain and its Empire really was and nor did they care. Keynes, a man dying from heart disease, eventually got a loan of $3.75 billion over fifty years at 2 per cent interest. It kept the wolf at bay but he would remain at Britain's door for a long time to come.

In such circumstances, it can be no surprise that the Liverpool authorities wanted the housing occupied by the Chinese. Nor, dreadful as it was for those concerned, should we be shocked

① Kynaston, D 'Austerity Britain; 1945 – 51', Bloomsbury Publishing, London, 2007, p.97.

战时跨大西洋联盟告一段落，大西洋两岸的国家现在都有了新的领导人。在杜鲁门切断英国的生命线不到1个月之前，由克莱门特·艾德礼领导的工党以压倒性优势获胜。面对危机，工党承诺实施大量的新政策，而且花费巨大。经济危机在工党政府执政期间一直持续着。英国在接下来的18个月里实际上处于破产状态，400万人将会离开军队系统，他们不得不去寻找新的工作。这些人以及他们的家人需要有住的地方，但英国当时住房严重短缺。尤其是像伦敦和利物浦这样遭到严重轰炸的城市，住房更加短缺。

刚刚执政的工党政府派出当时最杰出的经济学家凯恩斯勋爵来和美国人进行谈判。实际上，凯恩斯是去向美国乞讨，希望英国的战时同盟国兼财政施主国可以继续它的慷慨。凯恩斯想要60亿美元的无利息贷款，但英美两国的老交情随着罗斯福的去世已经终结了。美国人不知道英国经济那么萧条，而且他们对此也并不关心。死于心脏病的凯恩斯最终得到了37.5亿美元的贷款，期限为50年，并且有2%的利息。这样一来英国可以勉强维持下去，但从长远来看英国还是会面临危机。

在这样的情况下，利物浦政府想要中国人所占有的房屋也就不足为奇了。虽然对于那些当事人来说很糟糕，而且当这些中国人的家人陷入困境时也没有得到英国政府的“足够重视”，甚至连英国内政部也没有召开一场会议来商讨一下这件事。说

that the plight of their families was '...not seen to be sufficiently weighty...' to justify even a meeting at the Home Office to discuss it.[①] Sadly, officials and politicians saw themselves as facing far greater problems than the fate of a few hundred working class women and their mixed-race children.

12.2 Sex, racism or economics?

Havelock-Wilson, the head of the NSFU had been agitating about the Chinese for years. By 1908 his agitation had borne some fruit. An Act of Parliament of that year required that one in five Chinese mariners speak fluent English. Indian seamen were exempted from this requirement. And there were many more of them – over 50,000 by 1914.[②] More than ten times the number of Chinese employed in the British fleet. What was it about the Chinese that aroused the passions of the British mariners and their Union?

The problem with the Chinese mariners was that they were '... more sober and steady and do their work much more efficiently ...' than British seamen.[③] Unfortunately for him, the Chinese

① Note to file addressed to Mr Dudley, initialled AA, dated 27.9.46, File HO 213/926, National Archives, Kew, UK.

② Visram, R 'Asians in Britain: 400 Years of History', Pluto Press, London, 2002, p.54.

③ Quoted from 'Reynolds Newspaper', 23rd April, 1911, statement by Messrs Glen and Co. in 'Chinese Invasion of Great Britain: A National Danger. A Call to Arms. How British Labour Has Been Displaced by Cheap Chinese Asiatic Labour During the Last Twenty Years.' National Sailors and Firemen's Union Manning Committee, April 1914: MSS 175/3/16/2, Modern Records Centre, University of Warwick, UK.

来遗憾，官员和政客此刻正面临着更为严重的问题，比几百名工人阶层的女人和她们混血孩子的命运更为严重的问题。

第二节　性别、种族歧视还是经济因素?

英国水手及机工工会的领导者哈夫洛克－威尔逊数年来一直在中国海员问题上煽风点火。到了 1908 年，他的鼓动终于有所成效。议会颁布的一项法案要求每 5 名中国海员中需要有 1 名会说流利的英语，而印度海员则不需要遵循这项议会法案。这样一来印度海员就越来越多，截止到 1914 年，人数已经超过了 5 万。在英国船队上工作的印度海员比中国海员多出 10 倍还多。那么激起英国海员和其工会情绪的中国人到底是怎样的呢?

中国海员的状况是这样的：他们比起英国海员更为冷静和沉稳，工作效率更高。对英国海员来说，不幸的是，很多商船船长认为中国海员比欧洲海员好千百倍。也许最令人感到羞愧的是，英国女人似乎更喜欢中国海员。“当看到我们国家的女人与中国男人游荡在港口的街道上时，真令人感到羞愧和耻辱。”这些都引自一个代表英国海员意见的工会——英国水手及机工工会在 1914 年 4 月出版的一本小册子。事实上，工会承认中国海员更适合做海员，同时也是有担当的好男人，关键

seaman, as we saw earlier, was regarded by many merchant marine Captains as a seamen who '...when compared to the European is infinitely the better man.'① Perhaps most humiliating of all, the ladies seemed to prefer him. It was '...a crying shame and disgrace to see our own womenfolk tramping around the streets of our ports with Chinamen.'② These quotations all come from a pamphlet produced in April 1914 by the union representing British seamen, the National Sailors and Firemen's Union (NSFU). In effect, they concede that the Chinese men were better mariners and better men. Moreover, they were cheaper. They earned £2 a month if they were engaged in the Far East and only a little more, £3.10.0 (£3.50), if they signed on a ship in the UK. The British cost £5.10.0 (£5.50).

Perhaps worst of all, British women seemed to find them attractive. They were preferred marriage partners.

As we have seen, Havelock-Wilson continued his pressure for the ousting of the Chinese even during the First World War when the shortage of manpower was acute. With the end of the War the labour shortage vanished. In the summer of 1919 riots broke out in Liverpool and other major seaports throughout the country. The targets were the non-white seamen. All the fears and jealousies that

① Letter from Captain Froggart of the 'Indian Monarch', September 23rd, 1908, quoted in 'Chinese Invasion of Great Britain: A National Danger. A Call to Arms. How British Labour Has Been Displaced By Cheap Chinese Asiatic Labour During the Last Twenty Years.' National Sailors and Firemen's Union Manning Committee, April 1914: MSS 175/3/16/2, Modern Records Centre, University of Warwick, UK.

② 'Chinese Invasion of Great Britain: A National Danger. A Call to Arms. How British Labour Has Been Displaced By Cheap Chinese Asiatic Labour During the Last Twenty Years.' National Sailors and Firemen's Union Manning Committee, April 1914: MSS 175/3/16/2.

他们还很廉价。他们如果在远东船东的船上工作，每个月仅赚 2 英镑。如果在英国船东船上工作的话，每个月只多赚一点，即 3 英镑 10 先令（合 3.50 英镑）。而英国籍海员的薪资为每月 5 英镑 10 先令（合 5.50 英镑）。

对英国男人来说，也许最糟糕的是，英国女人似乎发现中国海员更有吸引力，是她们心中更合适的婚姻伴侣。

正如我们所看到的，哈夫洛克－威尔逊在持续施加压力，甚至在第一次世界大战劳动力严重短缺的情况下依然企图驱逐中国海员。随着战争的结束，劳动力短缺的现象逐渐消失。1919 年夏季，利物浦以及英国其他主要的港口发生暴乱，暴乱所针对的目标是那些非白种人的海员。多年以来，英国人内心充斥着的所有恐惧和嫉妒以一种无节制的暴力形式爆发出来。一来是为了和中国人竞争为数不多的工作机会，二来是他们的嫉妒心在作怪。英国海员嫉妒那些挣得少但似乎过得不错的中国海员，嫉妒那些抢走他们女人的中国人。

had simmered for years exploded in an orgy of violence. It was driven by the competition for scarce jobs and by jealousy. Jealousy of men who earned less but seemed to have a more prosperous life. Men who were taking 'their' women.①

The antipathy of the mariners and their union did not fade. It continued in the years between the wars and it continued after World War Two. As late as the mid-1970s there was blatant discrimination against non-white seamen in the British merchant marine. The Union was firm that their members would not accept '...the mixing of all colour and races ...on any ship.'② The employers were afraid to employ mixed crews.③ They feared that there was '...the real possibility (and in some cases, near certainty) of trouble on board...'④

Nothing much had changed in seventy-five years. Some members of white crews were still blatantly racist and bluntly refused to sail with non-white in the crews.⑤ The Union had changed its name but little else. It still wanted non-whites kept off the ships. They wanted British ships to employ British crews.⑥

① May, R and Cohen, R 'The Interaction Between Race and Colonialism: A Case Study of the Liverpool Race Riots of 1919' in Race and Class, vol. xvi, no. 2, 1974, pp. 111-126.

② Notes on Racial Discrimination, statement by National Union of Seamen; File MSS 175A No. 154, Modern Records Centre, University of Warwick, UK.

③ F. B. Bolton, President of the British Shipping Federation in 'The Observer' March 24th, 1974; File MSS 175A No. 154, Modern Records Centre, University of Warwick, UK.

④ Submission by the National Maritime Board to the Government on the possible Government Action on Racial Integration as applied to the Shipping Industry, January 8th, 1968, marked 'Confidential'; File MSS 175A No. 154, Modern Records Centre, University of Warwick, UK.

⑤ Note in File 175A No. 154 Modern Records Centre, University of Warwick, UK.

⑥ National Union of Seamen Paper NMB Asian Manning Meeting July 11th, 1973; File 175A No. 154 Modern Records Centre, University of Warwick, UK.

英国人一直对中国海员及其工会心存厌恶。这种厌恶感在第一次世界大战期间一直持续着，并且持续到“二战”之后。直到 20 世纪 70 年代中期，在英国商船上工作的非白种人的海员依然受到公然的歧视。英国海员工会的立场很坚定，声称其成员不能接受“在任何一艘船上混杂着其他肤色、其他种族的船员”。为了避免在船上出现麻烦，船东不敢雇佣其他人种的船员。

75 年过去了，这一切并没有太多的改变。一些白人海员依然是公然的种族歧视者，并直言不讳地拒绝与非白种人的海员一同航行。英国海员工会的名称虽然变了，但其他方面几乎没有改变。工会依然希望船上没有非白种人的海员，他们希望英国轮船只雇佣英国海员。

The Chinese seamen at the end of World War Two faced the same problems they had always faced since the beginning of the century. Problems they would continue to face for another thirty years. And they were now faced by a Government that saw itself as the representatives of the British working class. The end of World War Two saw a Labour Government in power. A Labour Government closely tied to the Unions. With millions of men looking for work and the memories of mass unemployment after the First World War, there would be little sympathy for the Chinese and their families in the halls of power.

12.3 Aggravation or the other

Mutual aid societies were part of everyday life in a Chinese community.[①] If a Chinese travelled to a place where he had never been before, he knew that he was not alone. As long as there were other Chinese, he could go to an organization that would help him. This might be composed of people from his own Province or district or one that boasted individuals all bearing the same family name. Faced with an employer, it was a very small step for him and his colleagues to form a trade union. If he came from Shanghai, he probably already had experience of union membership. Prior to the slaughter carried out by the Nationalists in 1927, that city had been

① C.S. Roberts, Secretary to the Colonial Advisory Committee: Trade Unionism in Malaya, April 1948; File MSS 292/959.1/2, Modern Records Centre, University of Warwick, UK.

“二战”结束以后，中国海员面临着从20世纪初期以来一直存在的问题。而且在接下来的三十年里，他们将会一直面临着这些问题。而现在，他们面对着这样一个将自己视为工人阶层代表的政府。“二战”结束时，英国工党政府执政。工党政府与工会联系紧密。伴随着大批英国人寻找工作，人们依然记得第一次世界大战过后大量的失业人口，因此，在权力面前，没有人会同情中国海员和他们的家人。

第三节　情况加剧还是其他

团体间的互帮互助是华人社区里人们日常生活的一部分。如果一名中国人到一个他从未去过的地方旅行，那他并不会感到孤单。因为只要那里有其他的中国人，他就可以找到能够帮助他的机构。机构里的人或许和他是同一个省或者同一个地区的，甚至也许在机构里他还能找到和他同姓的人。找到工作以后，这名中国人很容易就能和他的同事们一起组成一个工会。如果他来自上海，那他也许已经有参加工会的经历。在国民党1927年进行屠杀以前，上海曾经有300多家工会。

home to over three hundred unions.①

The Chinese seamen who came to Liverpool at the beginning of World War Two came to a city that already had an established infrastructure of Chinese organizations. The Chinese Freemasons Lodge already existed. Its members were Nationalist supporters. There was already a Chinese Seamen's Union in the city. It too was supported by the Nationalist Government, which had consular offices in the city.

Holt were concerned about the influence the Nationalist exerted on this Union but knew that this influence did not extend beyond the Cantonese seamen. The Shanghai men were completely outside of its influence.② Not a surprise given the linguistic differences between the Cantonese and Shanghainese and, as we have seen, their very different political sympathies.

Soon the Shanghai men would form the Communist Liverpool Chinese Seamen's Union. More than this they would have their own man at the very top of the Nationalist Union. S.E. Teh, Cambridge educated, and Secretary of the Nationalist Chinese Seamen's Union, was known to the British to be a Communist.③ His politics would be clear when he appeared in Hong Kong in 1947 as a member of a delegation from the Communist-backed

---

① British Labour Council for Chinese Freedom: Notes for Speakers No. 7, June 10th, 1927 New Trade Unions at Shanghai; File MSS 36-C74 China 1923-1972 Iron and Steel Trades Confederation 1886-1985, Modern Records Centre, University of Warwick, UK.

② Note to file, File M1839/43, National Archives, Kew, UK.

③ Note to file, File MT9/3692, National Archives, Kew, UK.

在"二战"开始时，利物浦的华人机构已经建立得很完善。中国共济会分会那时就已经建立了,其成员是国民党的支持者。利物浦还有一个中国海员工会，该工会也得到了国民党政府的支持，国民党在此设有领事办事处。

霍尔特担心国民党对中国海员工会有所影响，但他们也明白，即使有影响，这种影响也只能是在广东海员身上。上海海员完全不会受到国民党的影响。因为广东人和上海人不仅在语言上存在差异，另外他们的政治认同感也截然不同。

不久上海海员组成了由共产党领导的利物浦中国海员工会。除此之外，他们还在国民党工会的高层中安插了内线。剑桥大学毕业的郑锡恩是国民党中国海员工会的秘书，英国人后来才知道他也是共产党员。1947 年，当郑锡恩作为共产党支持的国际运输工人工会代表团的成员出现在香港时，人们才知道他真实的政治立场。在战争期间，郑锡恩作为间谍长期潜伏在国民党工会里。英国政府知道利物浦中国海员工会中的上海人和新加坡人与共产党有着密切的联系。

International Transport Workers Union.[1] For the duration of the War he would be the Communist mole in the Nationalist Union. The British authorities knew that the Liverpool Chinese Seamen's Union with its Shanghainese and Singaporean members was firmly linked to the Communist Party.[2]

Whether Nationalist or Communist, the Chinese seamen had, from the beginning of the War, fought hard for equality of treatment. Initially, the British Government, the Australian Government and the shipowners had tried physical force and the force of the law in an attempt to cow the men.[3] It did not work.

Unlike the Indian seamen who were outmanoeuvred by the shipowners and the British Government throughout the War,[4] the Chinese were well organised. What is more, they had an extremely able negotiator in the person of Dr. Wellington Koo. Even before their lengthy strike in 1942 the Chinese had come to be regarded as a '...constant source of aggravation...'[5]

They were all an aggravation and an irritation. But the Shanghai men seem to have been a particular thorn in the side of Alfred Holt and Company. Their stated determination to get rid

① 'Conversation with MR. H. E. Price', File 2342 2A Chinese Crews 1945-1955, Ocean Archive, Liverpool Maritime Museum, UK.

② Note to file, File MT9/3692, National Archives, Kew, UK.

③ Lane, Tony 'The Merchant Seamen's War', Manchester University Press, Manchester and New York, 1990, p. 164.

④ Visram, R 'Asians in Britain: 400 Years of History', Pluto Press, London, 2002, p.252.

⑤ Lane, Tony 'The Merchant Seamen's War', Manchester University Press, Manchester and New York, 1990, p. 163; Lane, Tony 'The Merchant Seamen's War', Manchester University Press, Manchester and New York, 1990, p. 164.

不论何时，中国海员从战争一开始就一直努力争取平等的待遇。最初，英国政府、澳大利亚政府以及船东尝试用武力以及法律手段来恐吓中国海员，但这并没有奏效。

1942年中国船员举行大罢工以前，船东和英国政府就把中国船员看作是“加剧冲突的长期存在的根源”。与战争期间受到船东和英国政府控制的印度海员不同，中国海员组织有序。另外，他们还有一位特别有能力的谈判专家，这个人就是顾维钧博士。

英国船东认为完全是中国海员加剧了冲突，激化了矛盾。站在阿尔弗雷德·霍尔特公司的立场上来看，上海海员就像是他们的眼中钉、肉中刺。霍尔特公司声称决心赶走上海海员，他们也许会得到英国政府的支持。上海海员成立的工会属于共产主义性质。第二次世界大战以前，共产党是英国政府主要的敌人。随着德国和日本的溃败，苏联红军用武力征服了欧洲东部的大部分区域，共产党再次成为英国的敌人。1946年3月，丘吉尔的“铁幕”演说标志着英国半官方地承认了共产主义实际上是西方世界不得不畏惧的敌人。

of the men would be likely to have been supported by the British Government. Their Union was Communist. The Communists were the main enemy before the Second World War. They rapidly became so again with the defeat of Germany and Japan. The Soviet Red Army had forcibly conquered much of Eastern Europe. Churchill's 'Iron curtain' speech of March 1946 marked the quasi-official acknowledgement that Communism was, indeed, the foe that the West had to fear.

The men who ran the Shanghai union would undoubtedly have been targeted for repatriation, as would any individual known to have been active in the Union. Perhaps this helps to explain why so many of those who were forced out were Shanghai men. Why we see in the case studies a link between being a Union activist or official and forced repatriation.

Nor would such men be likely to pay the bribes that at least one Holt employee demanded. Bribes to ensure that you got a ship, got the ship that you wanted or got the type of contract that you wanted.① Hardly surprising then that the men who landed in Shanghai had Nationalist officials waiting for them. Or that the Cantonese men on Fred Bishop's ship were Christians; also men who would not be likely to pay bribes.

12.4 Alfred Holt and Company

British shipping companies had had a very profitable war. In the four years leading to the outbreak of the conflict they had

① Stated in interviews with several old seamen and seamen's wives.

那些管理上海海员工会的海员们无疑是被遣返的对象，任何在工会里表现积极的人都将被遣返。这也许可以解释为什么在那些被遣返的海员中有那么多是上海海员了。这也可以解释为什么我们会在一些案例研究中发现工会的积极分子或工作人员都逃脱不了被迫遣返的命运。

如果中国海员肯向霍尔特公司的员工行贿，就可以保证登船，登上自己想上的船或是签下想要签的那类合同。所以，后来国民党官员能够提前获得消息在上海等待着那些登岸的海员也就不足为奇了。还有一种可能，在弗雷德·毕晓普的船上工作的广东海员是基督徒，他们即使有钱也不可能贿赂霍尔特公司的员工。

第四节　阿尔弗雷德·霍尔特公司

英国轮船公司在战争期间获利颇丰。在战争爆发的前四年里，英国轮船公司所赚的利润不超过其本金的 6%。而在战争

earned a return on their capital of no more than 6%. In the first three years of the war that figure rocketed. One firm realised a return on its invested capital of 30%, another an astounding 114% return on its assets.① In 1940 alone Holt had made a 26% profit on its operations.②

Yet, we have seen how Alfred Holt and Company was concerned about the competition they would face after the War. How the management of the company were '...anxious to press on with the general policy of manning all ships with fresh crews, on basic rates.'③ That is, get rid of the men who had by their own admission served them so well during the War and replace them with men on the lowest possible wages. Men who in many cases did not wish to go back 'home'. Holt knew this but decided to press on anyway.④

The men had to be transported back and Holt was determined that here too they would minimise their costs. They would try to use troopships to send men out to Hong Kong and use cargo vessels to move the Shanghai men on from Hong Kong to Shanghai. A good indication of how they viewed the men who had risked their

① Report from the Select Committee on National Expenditure: Session 1944-45, HMSO 1945; File OA 311 British Liner Committee, Ocean Archive, Liverpool Maritime Museum, UK.

② Ibidem.

③ Letter from Alfred Holt, Liverpool to Butterfield and Swire, Hong Kong and Singapore, March 15th, 1946; File 2342 Chinese Crews 1945 – 1955, Ocean Archive, Liverpool Maritime Museum, UK.

④ Letter from Alfred Holt and Company, Liverpool to Butterfield and Swire, Hong Kong dated November 2nd, 1945; File 2342 2A Chinese Crews 1945 – 1955, Ocean Archive, Liverpool Maritime Museum, UK.

爆发后的 3 年里，这一数字迅猛上涨。一家公司所获得的利润占其投资资金的 30%，另一家公司则达到了惊人的数字，其所获利润竟达到 114%。1940 年，仅霍尔特公司一家通过开展业务就获取了 26% 的利润。

我们已经了解了阿尔弗雷德·霍尔特公司非常关心他们在战后将会面临的竞争。我们也了解到公司的管理层“急于向员工施加新的政策，即为所有的船只配备最低薪水的新员工”。也就是要赶走那些公司曾承认在战争期间为其效力的海员，并且雇佣薪水最低的海员来替代他们。当然，海员们是不愿意回“家”的。霍尔特虽然知道这一点，但无论如何他都会实施新的政策。

中国海员们被迫遣返回国，而霍尔特竟然还打算在运输上尽可能地降低成本。公司计划使用军舰将这些海员先运送到香港，接下来使用货船将上海的海员从香港再运送到上海。很显然，他们将那些曾冒着生命危险为公司以及大英帝国工作的海员们视为了货物。在此次行程中，这些上海海员的容身之处就是“150 吨货物所腾出的空间”。“将轮船中后部的船舱空出来之后，可以容纳另外的 100 名乘客，这些地方也没有经过任何装修。”我们无法想象这些海员在漫长的航程中坐在哪里、怎样坐；睡在哪里、怎样睡。

lives for them and for the United Kingdom – cargo. All that would be involved in accommodating the Shanghai men on their trip would be '...shifting about 150 tons of ...cargo...' Then the vessels '...could accommodate a further 100 passengers in the after centre-castle, without fittings'.① One wonders where and how the men were to sit, or to sleep.

By the beginning of January 1946 Holt ships were leaving full of the men being forced out of the country. The Public Records Office at Kew in the UK holds the crew lists for many of these ships. Each of the vessels taking the men out of the country is marked as taking the men to '... such a port in Malaya, Hong Kong or China from which repatriation is possible.'

The 'Ajax' left Birkenhead on January 3rd 1946. On board were a small number of so-called supernumerary crew. Amongst these were Second Mate W. Shu Chung and a lady – S.K. Lee, a supernumerary stewardess. Both were heading back to their home in Shanghai. For both of them this was 812 Rue Bourget. An address in the French Concession in that city. Since Chinese women do not change their family name on marriage, were they a married couple? How long had they been in the UK? Perhaps they were happy to go back. Or perhaps they were amongst the many who did not want to go. Like the married men who had been

① Letter from Alfred Holt, Liverpool to Butterfield and Swire, Hong Kong and Singapore, March 15th, 1946; File 2342 Chinese Crews 1945 – 1955, Ocean Archive, Liverpool Maritime Museum, UK.

1946 年 1 月初，霍尔特的船上满载着被迫遣返回国的中国海员。位于英国基尤的公共档案办公室存有很多艘船上的海员名单。每一艘负责遣返任务的船都有类似“海员可被遣返到马来西亚、香港或是中国的港口上”的备注。

1946 年 1 月 3 日，“阿伽克斯”号驶离了伯肯黑德。船上有一小部分额外的船员。在这些人中有二副 W. 舒钟（W. Shu Chung）以及一位名叫 S.K. 李的女服务员。这两个人都在驶向他们位于上海的家——布尔热街 812 号，一个曾经是上海法租界的地址。由于中国女人结婚后不会改变姓氏，那么他们俩是一对已婚的夫妇吗？他们在英国待了多久？他们也许很高兴能够回国。又或许他们也是很多不想离开英国的人中的一员。与那些被列入黑名单的已婚男人一样，他们同样拿到的是单程票，返回中国后便再也回不来了。

blacklisted, they too were on a one-way ticket 'home'.①

The ships continued to stream out of the River Mersey. The 'Menestheus' left on 25th January② and soon Holt began to use the vessels of its associated companies to speed up the process. The 'Lyidon' of China Mutual left the UK on 15th March heading for Hong Kong.③ And so it continued until July 1946 when the last repatriation ship we can trace, China Mutual's 'Asphalion', steamed off to the Far East.④

Holt had got rid of the men but its troubles had not evaporated. The company now faced a hostile workforce. The removal of the War Risk Bonus led to strikes of Holt crew in Australia. Any savings they thought they had made were lost as they conceded significant pay increases simply to get the ships moving.⑤ And more problems were to follow over the next two years.

Significantly, other employers certainly did not think Holt's removal of the Bonus was justified.⑥ Anglo-Saxon Petroleum had

① Chinese Crew, Agreement and List of the Crew, MV 'Ajax'; File BT 381/3915, National Archives, Kew, UK.

② Chinese Crew, Agreement and List of the Crew, MV 'Menestheus'; File BT 381/390, National Archives, Kew, UK.

③ Chinese Crew, Agreement and List of the Crew, MV 'Lyidon'; File BT 381/3793, National Archives, Kew, UK.

④ Chinese Crew, Agreement and List of the Crew, MV 'Asphalion'; File BT381/3855, National Archives, Kew, UK.

⑤ Letter Butterfield and Swire, Sydney to Alfred Holt and Company, Liverpool, dated November 14th, 1946; File 2342 2A Chinese Crews 1945 – 1955, Ocean Archive, Liverpool Maritime Museum, UK.

⑥ Resolution at meeting of June 24th, 1945, NVS Finance and General Purposes Committee; File MSS 178/1/2/18 NVS Finance and General Purposes Committee, Modern Records Centre, Warwick University, UK.

霍尔特的船继续驶离默西河。1 月 25 日，“梅内斯特斯”号驶离默西河，不久之后霍尔特开始征用其联合公司的船来加快运送中国海员回国。3 月 15 日，中国协力轮船公司的“林登”号离开英国驶向香港。遣返工作一直持续到 1946 年 7 月，我们可以追溯到的最后一艘遣返中国海员的轮船是中国协力轮船公司的“艾丝凡兰”号。

霍尔特虽然清除了中国海员，但公司的麻烦却并没有消除。由于公司取消了员工的战时津贴，对此严重不满的员工们在澳大利亚举行了罢工。公司通过雇佣廉价船员所节省下的所有费用最后都花掉了，正如他们所承认的那样，仅仅是让船只再次开航就花费了更高的费用。而且在接下来的两年里，公司将面临着更多的麻烦。

更有意思的是，其他船东也不认可霍尔特公司取消战时津贴的决定。壳牌石油公司就没有这样做，而且也没有将员工驱逐出境。1946 年 7 月，壳牌石油公司依然在英国签约或是解约海员，并且依然支付给员工每个月 10 英镑的战时津贴。到了 1947 年，甚至连霍尔特也不得不承认：由于白人海员还享有奖金，我们没有理由歧视中国海员。霍尔特的这一坦白也表明公司削减员工薪资的举措导致了很多问题。

not done it. Nor were they acting to force men out of the country. Shell Oil was still signing on and discharging men in the UK in July 1946 and the company was still paying them the £10 a month War Risk Bonus.① By 1947 even Holt was having to concede that, given that white crews were still receiving the Bonus, there was no '...defensible reason for the discrimination.'② An admission that had much to do with the problems that their cost-cutting actions had now caused for them.

Holt's anxiety to keep their labour costs as low as possible had led them to do more than just remove the Bonus. They had also reduced their pay rates to a level where, according to their agents Butterfield and Swire, men in Shanghai could not support their families.③ Holt were now paying a big price for their parsimony. Men they were willing to sign simply refused to join the Company's ships. By the end of 1946 Holt was finding it virtually impossible to recruit seamen.④ They would not take on the men they had dismissed at the end of the War and they could not get

① Letter from Anglo-Saxon Petroleum, London W1 to Ministry of Transport, dated July 4th, 1946; File MT 9/4446 Anglo-Saxon Petroleum Co Ltd: Seamen's Home – Chinese Seamen's Articles [revision to pre-war operation of the fleet], National Archives, Kew, UK.

② Letter from Alfred Holt, Liverpool 1 to Butterfield and Swire Hong Kong and Shanghai, dated January 3rd, 1947; File 2342 2A Chinese Crews 1945 – 1955, Ocean Archive, Liverpool Maritime Museum, UK.

③ Letter from JFV Robinson for Butterfield and Swire as Blue Funnel, Hong Kong to JCL Wong, Holt's Wharf, Kowloon; File 2342 2A Chinese Crews 1945 – 1955, Ocean Archive, Liverpool Maritime Museum, UK.

④ Letter from Butterfield and Swire, Hong Kong to Alfred Holt and Company, Liverpool, dated November 14th, 1946; File 2342 2A Chinese Crews 1945 – 1955, Ocean Archive, Liverpool Maritime Museum, UK.

霍尔特急于降低员工的劳动报酬，公司不仅取消了员工的战时津贴，而且减少了员工的基本工资。根据公司的代理太古轮船公司所说，薪水已经低到了让上海的海员都无法养活他们家人的地步。霍尔特为他们的吝啬付出了沉重的代价，原本有意签约的海员直接拒绝与霍尔特公司续约。战争结束后被解雇的船员，公司不能继续雇佣，而又找不到其他海员。到了 1946 年年底，霍尔特发现公司很难再雇佣到海员了。1947 年 4 月，他们最终作出了让步。大台服务员的薪资从一个月 14 英镑 7 先令（合 14.35 英镑）上涨为 21 英镑 19 先令（合 21.95 英镑），机工的薪资从 9 英镑 2 先令（合 9.10 英镑）上涨为 13 英镑 13 先令（合 13.65 英镑），即我们之前提到的上涨 50% 的薪资。

any others. In April 1947 they finally conceded defeat.① A Chief Steward's pay went from £14.7.0 (£14.35) a month to £21.19.0 (£21.95); a Donkeyman in a ship's engine room from £9.2.0 (£9.10) to £13.13.0 (£13.65). The 50% increase we talked about earlier.

Holt may have got rid of its 'agitators' but it had saved little or no money in the process. The main result of their actions was the destruction of the lives of hundreds of Anglo-Chinese families in Liverpool. Alfred Holt had created Liverpool's unique Chinese community. Now they had all but destroyed it.

It was never to be the same again.

This original community that was an integral part of Liverpool would be forgotten as waves of migrants came in to Liverpool. Predominantly from Hong Kong's New Territories, they would come as family groups. Their menfolk would not seek their partners amongst Liverpool's white working class. There would be few Eurasian children. For the first time, there would be a Chinatown largely isolated from the society that surrounded it.

① Report on Blue Funnel Conference, Singapore April 1st, 1947; File 2342 2A Chinese Crews 1945 – 1955, Ocean Archive, Liverpool Maritime Museum, UK.

霍尔特也许摆脱了所谓的“闹事儿的人”，但公司在这个过程中只节省了很少的费用，或者说根本没有节省费用。公司的举措所造成的主要结果就是毁掉了生活在利物浦的无数中英结合家庭的生活。阿尔弗雷德·霍尔特曾经创造了利物浦独特的华人社区，现在却差一点摧毁了它，华人社区再也不能和从前一样了。

随着大批新移民陆续不断地来到利物浦，曾是利物浦一部分的早期华人社区也会被人们遗忘。新的移民绝大多数来自香港新界，而且他们是以家庭为单位移民到这里。这些移民中的男子不太会在利物浦白人的工薪阶层里寻找伴侣，因此这里也就不会有那么多欧亚混血的孩子了。利物浦将第一次出现一个在很大程度上与周围社区隔绝的唐人街。